VW Kübelwagen/ Schwimmwagen

VW Type 82 Kübelwagen (1940–45)/VW Type 128/166 Schwimmwagen (1942–44)

COVER PHOTOGRAPHS: Main picture –
restored VW Type 82 Kübelwagen;
insets – restored Type 166 Schwimmwagen.

First published in May 2015

A catalogue record for this book is available
from the British Library.

ISBN 978 0 85733 779 5

Library of Congress control no. 2014953498

Published by Haynes Publishing,
Sparkford, Yeovil,
Somerset BA22 7JJ, UK.
Tel: 01963 442030 Fax: 01963 440001
Int. tel: +44 1963 442030
Int. fax: +44 1963 440001
E-mail: sales@haynes.co.uk
Website: www.haynes.co.uk

Haynes North America Inc.,
861 Lawrence Drive, Newbury Park,
California 91320, USA.

Printed in the USA by Odcombe Press LP,
1299 Bridgestone Parkway, La Vergne,
TN 37086.

Acknowledgements

Several people have given me invaluable help in the production
of this book. First and foremost, I must thank Oliver Barnham,
for his tireless assistance in providing indispensable research
materials on both the Kübelwagen and Schwimmwagen, plus
access to his own restored Type 82. He also consulted on the
manuscript, although any mistakes are purely my own. Without his
help, and his trusting me with rare documents and publications,
writing this book would have been a far more arduous affair, and I
extend my deepest gratitude. Thanks also go to Bruce Crompton,
Max Crompton and Phil Rutherford, for explaining to me the
vehicles and components in Bruce's astonishing vehicle collection
(www.axistrackservices.com). With regard to sourcing photographs,
I acknowledge the help of the Bundesarchiv, the Porsche Museum,
Volkswagen Museum and Cody Images. Finally, I would like to
thank Jonathan Falconer of Haynes Publishing, for commissioning
me to write the book and for his always professional and friendly
assistance with several Haynes projects.

VW Kübelwagen/ Schwimmwagen

VW Type 82 Kübelwagen (1940–45)/VW Type 128/166 Schwimmwagen (1942–44)

Enthusiasts' Manual

Insights into the design, construction and operation of Germany's classic Second World War military utility vehicles

Dr Chris McNab

WH-1275659

Contents

6	Introduction	

8	Development	

The people's car	11
The military vehicle	13
War variants	17
The Schwimmwagen	19
Post-war life	23
Type 181	24
VW Country Buggy	26
Enthusiasts	27

28	Basic design and features	

Basic engine/transmission layout	30
Suspension and shock absorbers	33
Steering system	35
Brakes	35
Tyres and wheels	37
Bodywork and windscreen	37
Electrical systems	41
Lighting	42
Schwimmwagen amphibious system	43
Amphibious propulsion	46

50	The engine and transmission	

Crankcase and crankshaft	52
Pistons, camshaft and cylinders	53
Lubrication	54
Air cooling and cleaning	55
Ignition system	56
Gearbox	59
Differential	62

64	In war and peace	

Reconnaissance vehicles	67
The Kübelwagen and Schwimmwagen in combat	71
Weapons fitment	75
Combat crews	78
Allied analysis	83
Post-war runners	90

96	The driver's view	

The driver's role	98
Instruments	101
Driving characteristics	107
Schwimmwagen – amphibious driving	110
Driving experience	114
Extreme conditions	118
The driver's burden	125

126	The engineer's view	

Operational maintenance	128
Environmental problems	132
Cold-climate maintenance	138
Major component maintenance	139
Gearbox and differential	140
Engine removal	143
Engine installation	144

146	Appendix	

Kübelwagen Troubleshooting Guide – US War Department manual	146

153	Bibliography	

154	Index	

OPPOSITE This VW Type 82 Kübelwagen 'Trop' was built in 1942 and served in North Africa with the 164. *Leichte Afrika* Division, in whose markings it has been restored by military vehicle collector Oliver Barnham. *(Courtesy Oliver Barnham)*

Introduction

BELOW A German paratrooper in Italy, 1944, puts a Type 166 through its paces. The short grab handle on the body indicates that this vehicle is an early model; later models had the handle extending from wing to wing. *(Oliver Barnham)*

In January 1943, Allied forces fighting in the sand-blown expanses of North Africa came across a humble-looking German light infantry vehicle, amidst hundreds left stranded by the retreating *Deutsch-Italienische Panzerarmee* (German-Italian Panzer Army) on its flight westwards. The intriguing vehicle – a Type 82 Kübelwagen – was already a familiar shape to the British soldier, but there remained an eagerness to study its engineering and performance in greater detail. Therefore, this particular Type 82 made the long journey from North Africa to the British Midlands, for assessment by the British Intelligence Objectives Sub-committee (BIOS).

The findings contained within this report will be studied in detail throughout this book, yet the final paragraph of the report's Introduction merits quotation as a summary:

Looking at the general picture, we do not consider that the design represents any special brilliance, apart from certain of the detail points, and it is suggested that it is not to be regarded as an example of first class modern design to be copied by the British industry.

(BIOS, 1946, p. 10)

The quotation is deeply infused with a patronising tone, and a reluctance to see the vehicle properly in context. For as we shall see,

the Kübelwagen and its amphibious derivative, the Type 166 Schwimmwagen, were extremely intelligent pieces of engineering, when viewed in their full historical setting.

From a technological perspective, the Third Reich is rightly known for its general tendency towards over-complex experimentation. While Hitler's engineers advanced every aspect of military design during the 1930s and the war years, the overproliferation of types and the expense of the research process undoubtedly distracted from making more prosaic but valuable investments in the arsenal. The Type 82 and Type 166, however, stand as definite exceptions. While not carrying the glamour of a Tiger tank, a Messerschmitt Me 262 or a Type XXI U-boat, the Kübelwagen and Schwimmwagen were perfectly suited to military and industrial requirements, delivering the right product specification to perform an important battlefield role. Some 50,435 Type 82s were produced between 1940 and 1945,

and 14,283 Type 166s. From the ice-locked landscapes of a Ukrainian winter, to the scalding Saharan desert of Libya, through to the mud of autumnal Italy and benign summer months in France, the Kübelwagen was to be seen, reliably serving its soldiery. Above everything, the dependability and simplicity of these vehicles are the true marks of their success.

This book will explore the Kübelwagen and Schwimmwagen's technical and tactical history in detail, revealing what made them remarkable vehicles and why they were valued by those who used them. The story extends right up to the present day, for a thriving Kübelwagen and Schwimmwagen subculture still exists. Around the world, hundreds of Kübelwagens and rather fewer Schwimmwagens, faithfully restored, regularly run along European or American streets or show off their capabilities at military fairs. Why this rather basic vehicle should endure is, at heart, the story of this book.

BELOW An extremely clean-looking Luftwaffe Kübelwagen, the arm of service indicated by the 'WL' prefix on the number plate. *(Oliver Barnham)*

Chapter One

Development

The Kübelwagen and Schwimmwagen were born out of Germany's intensive militarisation during the 1930s, and its war requirements from 1939. Yet its origins actually lie in that most iconic of civilian cars – the Volkswagen (VW) Beetle.

OPPOSITE A nicely restored modern Kübelwagen. The painted panel on the door is the *Nutzlast Deckel*, which provided basic weights and classification information about the vehicle. *(AlfvanBeem)*

RIGHT The
brains behind the
Kübelwagen –
Ferdinand Porsche,
one of the greatest
automotive engineers
of the 20th century.
(BArch)

BELOW Adolf Hitler
makes an address
at the laying of the
foundation stone
of the Volkswagen
factory at Fallersleben,
26 May 1938.
Ferdinand Porsche
stands to the extreme
right of the picture.
(BArch)

The Kübelwagen's development began
during one of the most remarkable and
threatening renaissances in history. When
the First World War ended in 1918, Germany
was an industrially gutted and politically
fractured nation. The Versailles Treaty
hobbled German military redevelopment
at every level, placing strict limits upon
its human and material expansion for
the future. Periods of hyperinflation and
economic unrest left millions struggling on
the brink of poverty, or cast into long-term
unemployment or under-employment.

Into this turmoil stepped Adolf Hitler, a
virulently anti-Semitic former soldier who,
through fortuitous timing and a charismatic
personality, built up his Nationalsozialistische
Deutsche Arbeiterpartei (NSDAP) until he
and it took the reins of power in Germany in
1933. He then cemented that power through
an astonishing rebirth of German military and
industrial strength. The Versailles Treaty's
conditions were rejected, and the new,
formidable Wehrmacht emerged in 1935,
replacing the previous Reichswehr. Massive
public spending resulted in near full employment
and a highly visible rise in the standard of living.
Between 1932 and 1938, the German gross
domestic product (GDP) grew by 11% per
annum, fuelling almost celebratory consumption
of every type of product and service. It is
little wonder that many of the German people
embraced, or overlooked, the fact that they
were living in a Nazi dictatorship.

Motoring was also a beneficiary of the Nazi
investment, not least in the famous autobahn
road network. Although the idea of an extensive
national road network was by no means
Hitler's idea (planning had actually begun
during the 1920s), he turned the idea into a
reality through the efforts of 400,000 workers
and supply chain personnel, headed by Fritz
Todt as Generalinspektor für das deutsche
Straßenwesen (General Inspector for German
Roadways). Thus, when Hitler took power as
the German Chancellor in 1933, there were
just 108km (67 miles) of autobahn; by 1939
there were 3,300km (2,050 miles). Similarly,
car ownership in the early 1930s was the
preserve of the rich. This was about to change.
The Great Depression had almost obliterated

Fahrgestell des KdF-Wagens mit aufmontierten Vordersitzen, von oben gesehen

the German car industry (only 12 of 86 auto companies survived this period), but those that did make it through began to supply motor-minded German citizens with an ever-growing range of vehicles. Some of these companies were American-owned – principally Ford and Opel (a subsidiary of General Motors) – but they also included home-grown talent such as Daimler-Benz, Horch, Dampf Kraft Wagen (DKW), Wanderer and Audi. (The last four companies on this list formed the Auto Union AG in 1932, and went on to become one of the powerhouses of German vehicle production during the 1930s.) Through the output of these companies, plus the rise in wages, automobile ownership tripled in Germany during the 1930s. Yet Hitler had a more unified vision of how to get the German people moving, and here we begin the story of the Kübelwagen.

The people's car

It is a deep irony that the Volkswagen Beetle, a car most associated with the 'love and peace' generation of the 1960s, should have been born under one of history's most pernicious dictatorships. The name behind what would become the Volkswagen Type 1 (the Beetle) was the great Ferdinand Porsche. Having been practically involved in automobile design since the late 1890s (see biographical

feature on p. 12), Porsche rapidly became one of Germany's most innovative engineers. In 1931, working alongside the Zündapp company, Porsche developed the Type 12 *Auto für Jedermann* (Car for Everybody). The car did not make it much past the concept stage – only three prototypes had been manufactured by 1932 – but the curvaceous profile of the Type 1 was in evidence, if not the engineering (the Type 12 had a five-cylinder radial engine and swing-axle rear suspension).

Although the Type 12 would not become a production vehicle, in 1933 Porsche, now head of his own design office, met Hitler at the Hotel Kaiserhof in Munich. Both men were energised at the concept of creating an affordable, reliable, fuel-efficient and serviceable car for the German masses. Hitler shaped the proposition in more detail, throwing down a challenge to Porsche. Hitler envisaged a car capable of carrying five people at sustained speeds of 100km/h, and with a maximum fuel economy of 7 litres for every 100km travelled (or 33mpg). Hitler had even costed the new vehicle in his mind – it should not exceed 1,000RM, a figure that made Porsche blanch.

On 22 June 1934, Porsche received his commission to begin development of the car in earnest, leaning on the established profile of the Type 12 for his inspiration. Porsche also appears to have drawn on the designs of Hans

Ledwinka, designer for the Czech Tatra concern – in fact, in 1961 VW paid a total out-of-court settlement of 3 million DM to Ringhoffer-Tatra to settle copyright suits. This development phase was one of the most costly automobile

projects in history, as Porsche – who was very much on Hitler's list of approved individuals – had almost limitless access to the Reich's coffers. Prototypes emerged throughout 1935 and 1936, with much of the testing focused on three 'Type 60 V3' prototypes produced by October 1936. (The VW Beetle only took the 'Type 1' designation in the post-war years.) On this basis, 30 'W3' models were produced by Daimler-Benz to facilitate more extensive testing. The tests were exhaustive, and cost 30 million RM, but the expenditure was at least bearing fruit. What was emerging was a car of impressive simplicity and intelligent design. The curved style of the Type 12 remained, allied to a rear-mounted 986cc, 23.5hp flat-four engine, which was air-cooled rather than water-cooled. In terms of suspension, Porsche rejected the use of coil or leaf springs in favour of torsion bar suspension. The vehicle had an independent steel floorplan that meant the chassis could virtually be driven by itself; the bodywork was effectively a non-load-bearing bolt-on extra, which had important implications for the vehicle's future development. All told, Porsche had more than fulfilled his brief.

The completed Type 60 was unveiled to Hitler in 1937, and he was more than satisfied with what he saw. Now the major challenge

FERDINAND PORSCHE

Born on 3 September 1875, the son of a plumbing business owner, Ferdinand Porsche showed an obsessive relationship with engineering from his teenage years. After earning an apprenticeship as a plumber, he later entered employment with several engineering companies, in which he showed precocious talent in automobile engineering. By 1906 he had risen to become the Technical Manager at Austro-Daimler in Wiener Neustadt, and by 1917 he was General Manager with responsibility for a range of sophisticated heavy trucks and aero engines. During the 1920s Porsche was at the forefront of high-performance engine design, working for Daimler-Motoren-Gesellschaft and Steyr-Werke AG. The Technische Hochschule (Institute of Technology) in Stuttgart also conferred the honorary title of Dr. Ing. (Doctor of Engineering) on Porsche after the victory of his Mercedes vehicle in the Targa Florio race. In 1931, Porsche set up his own independent design office, and created one of history's most successful civilian vehicles, the Volkswagen Beetle, plus numerous other ground-breaking designs. Porsche became a general manager at Volkswagen GmbH. At the end of the war in 1945, Porsche was arrested by the French and spent nearly two years in prison, although he returned to car design on his release. He died in Stuttgart in 1951, aged 75.

was how to take this vehicle to the masses. Even given the German industrial 'miracle', this was no easy matter. Not only did the Type 60 not have a production plant, but Germany itself did not possess the automobile mass-production expertise exhibited by the likes of Henry Ford in the United States. (Porsche personally went to the United States to study the American production methods.) What was needed was funding, and lots of it. The coffers were opened courtesy of the Kraft durch Freude (KdF; Strength through Joy) organisation. Essentially a National Socialist tourism and leisure group, operating within the Deutsche Arbeitsfront (DAF; German Labour Front), the KdF took official charge of promoting the virtues of the Type 60 to the masses, while also using its huge financial resources to establish, on 1 July 1938, a vast Volkswagen works near Fallersleben, Lower Saxony, called Stadt des KdF-Wagens bei Fallersleben (City of the KdF Car at Fallersleben). Average Germans would have the chance to own a 'KdF-Wagen', as the new vehicle was labelled, via a special savings programme. A suggested deduction from salary of 5RM per week would ostensibly bring the saver the 990RM car in four years. The scheme was vigorously promoted and equally vigorously adopted – some 336,668 people paid into the scheme, the total contribution being 280 million RM. It appeared that Hitler's vision of national car ownership was becoming a reality.

The military vehicle

All those who sank their money into the KdF-Wagen saving scheme would be cruelly disappointed – not one of them would receive their vehicle. By the time the Second World War broke out in 1939, just 210 KdF-Wagens had been produced, these going into the eager hands of wealthy industrialists or the Nazi elite. (Contra the model of a vehicle affordable for all, the average buying price for one of these pre-war vehicles was around 8,000RM.) As to the rest of Germany, the war took precedence over their personal freedom.

Furthermore, development of the KdF-Wagen was already exploring a different route. The origins of this journey lay back in 1934. Various members of the Reich Chancellery and

Waffen-SS/Army representatives, in discussions with Porsche about his new vehicle, issued a report in which they not only stated the civilian requirements of the car, but also expressed the possibility that it might 'meet the military demands of carrying three men, one machine gun, and ammunition once the body has been removed'. The design of the Type 60, with its independent chassis, made the bodywork conversion of the car into a military vehicle a distinct option. This option was sharpened up through a report on 14 January 1938 from SS Hauptsturmführer Albert Liese, head of the VW motor pool and a Type 60 test driver, to the chief of the Heereswaffenamt (HWA; Army Weapons Office), General der Infanterie Kurt Liese. The SS officer outlined the possibilities of a light military vehicle based upon the VW chassis, and the general was intrigued enough to commission one Oberstleutnant Fichtner to work with Liese to establish the army's requirements and to produce something more concrete.

The VW design bureau had its work cut out. It had to design a vehicle that was fundamentally reliable in battlefield conditions, easy to maintain and with a low thirst for fuel. It had to operate convincingly both on-road and off-road, and in terrain varying from the tropical

ABOVE The motorcycle and sidecar combination was a major component of the Wehrmacht's reconnaissance force in the early years of the war. Over time the Kübelwagen and Schwimmwagen replaced many of them in front-line service. *(BArch)*

ABOVE A Type 82 pauses during operations in the North African desert in 1942. Note the large, smooth-tread 'balloon' tyres specially designed for desert travel. (BArch)

BELOW German soldiers in winter uniforms conduct a briefing on the front body of their Schwimmwagen in the Eastern Front. (Nik Cornish at www.stavka.org.uk)

to the arctic. It had to have a ground clearance of 240mm (9.4in) under the centre of the vehicle, and a turning radius of just 8m (26ft). Crucially – for reasons of both manoeuvrability and economy – it had to be light. It was calculated by the HWA that the vehicle could have a total off-road weight of 950kg (2,090lb), of which 400kg (880lb) was given to the chassis and tyre weight; four soldiers carrying all their kit deducted another 400kg (880lb). This meant that the total weight for the body was just 150kg (330lb), a significant material challenge given that the bodies of existing German light vehicles tended to weigh in the region of 300–400kg (660–880lb). The challenge of designing this economical body went to the coachbuilding firm Trutz.

Development and testing of the new vehicle proceeded rapidly, once the green light was given on 1 February 1938 to produce the first prototype. It emerged under the name *Kübelwagen* – 'bucket car'. This term, which would stick throughout the vehicle's lifetime, came from the bucket-like design of the vehicle's seating. In fact, the original name for the vehicle was the *Kübelsitzwagen* (bucket-seat car), a label actually applied to a broader spectrum of German military cars, but this was shortened for ease of use and attached to a very specific vehicle.

The military prototypes of the Kübelwagen were eventually, in 1939, given the official nomenclature of Type 62. Although the overall weight requirements were met, off-road performance and ground clearance, however, still did not quite satisfy the prescribed standards and the work continued. Further issues emerged when the Type 62 prototypes were combat tested during the campaign in Poland in September 1939. Here the Kübelwagen began to establish its worth, showing itself as rugged, manoeuvrable and capable of enduring thousands of miles of duty. There were problems, nonetheless. It must be remembered that the German Army was only partially mechanised; much of its soldiery still marched into battle on their feet. The gearing of the Type 62 was too fast for the Kübelwagen to accompany marching soldiers, so the gearing was adjusted to achieve a lowest speed of 4km/h (2.5mph). At the same time, the introduction of gear-reduction hubs increased the vehicle's

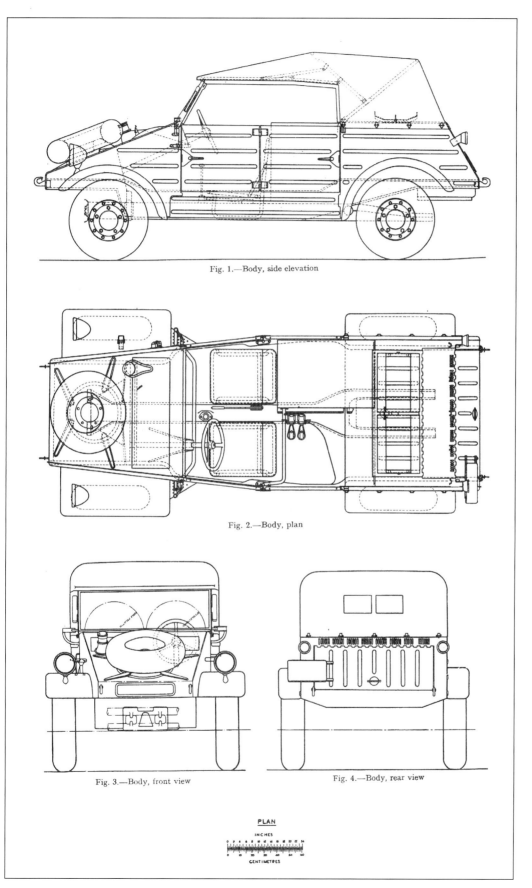

Fig. 1.—Body, side elevation

Fig. 2.—Body, plan

Fig. 3.—Body, front view

Fig. 4.—Body, rear view

PLAN

INCHES

CENTIMETRES

LEFT A detailed
engineering diagram
of the Kübelwagen
assessed by the British
Humber engineers.
Note the excellent
ground clearance in
the front view. *(Crown
Copyright)*

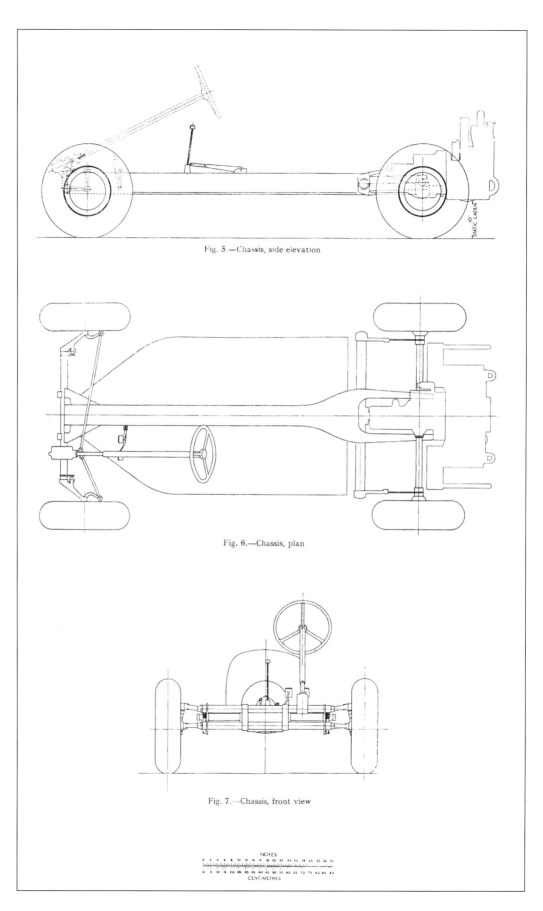

Fig. 5.—Chassis, side elevation

Fig. 6.—Chassis, plan

Fig. 7.—Chassis, front view

INCHES

CENTIMETRES

ground clearance and delivered more torque, while the use of a positive-locking differential gave four-wheel-drive type performance over rough ground even though the car was two-wheel drive. The angular body was further refined, made out of stamped sheet steel panels.

What emerged from the period of testing and further development was the definitive Kübelwagen – the Type 82 – which entered production at some point between May and August 1940. The improvements over the Type 62 had produced a vehicle perfectly suited to the demands of a field army in multiple theatres. The combination of its light weight, limited slip differential, reduction gears in the rear wheel hubs and independent suspension on all wheels meant that it could negotiate terrains where other vehicles would grind to a halt. An air-cooled engine significantly reduced the possibility of overheating in hot climates or freezing up in cold environments, and also avoided vehicle-stopping incidents of radiators being pierced by bullets. The car was simple to operate and repair, and gave good ground clearance of around 280mm (11in). Furthermore, because the body itself was not weight bearing, it could be changed easily to repurpose the vehicle in-theatre. Fuel economy had been achieved – just 8 litres (1.8 imp. gallons) of fuel were needed to take the car and four occupants over a distance of 100km (62 miles). Porsche and VW had created a winning combination.

War variants

Although, as we shall see, the Allies were somewhat sniffy about the Kübelwagen's capabilities when compared to their own vehicles, there is little objective argument against the Type 82's excellence as an infantry vehicle. This was proved by the functionality of the car in a huge range of theatre types. Between 1940 and 1945, the Kübelwagen operated successfully in the blistering desert conditions of North Africa, the mountainous terrain of Italy and the Balkans, the paralysing Soviet winters in Russia and the Ukraine, and the temperate zone variability of western Europe.

As well as transporting hundreds of thousands of humble German soldiers across the battlefield, the Type 82 also became the vehicle of choice for many staff officers. Erwin Rommel, for example, renowned leader of the Deutsche Afrika Korps (DAK), actually credited a Kübelwagen with saving his life during the North Africa campaign. As he explained the situation to Porsche himself, he had been in a Kübelwagen when he accidentally found himself in an enemy minefield. Such was the light weight of the car that it did not detonate an anti-tank mine as the vehicle's wheels passed over it. The much heavier Horch car following Rommel was not so lucky – it was blown to pieces when it came into contact with the underground charge.

The tactical challenges of a war, fought across so many theatres, plus the environmental testing that came with such diverse deployments, meant that the Type 82 was trialled in a multitude of variants in its four short years of war service. Some variants were matters of simple upgrades to key features – in March 1943 the 985cc Type 82 received a more powerful 1,131cc engine, taking the power up to the 25bhp originally intended for the KdF-Wagen. However, it was the Kübelwagen's body conversions that really gave the vehicle its battlefield flexibility. In addition to being a simple four-seat infantry car, it could be modified in a variety of ways.

BELOW Kübelwagens in production at Fallersleben. In total, 50,435 Type 82s were built between 1940 and 1945. *(Author's collection)*

THE TYPE 157 KÜBELWAGEN

An interesting diversion for the Kübelwagen was the Type 157 rail-capable vehicle. Here was essentially a standard Type 82, but with specially adapted wheels that enabled it to run on railway lines with a total track width of less than 1,435mm (56.5in). Conversion of a regular Kübelwagen into a rail-capable vehicle took just 8–12 minutes in the hands of a well-trained crew, the process involving jacking up the car and fitting steel rail wheels alongside the regular tyres; the rail wheels formed inner flanges that secured the car to the rails. The rail wheels themselves could be stored under the spare wheel, and individually weighed just 15kg (33lb). However, although many rail cars relied purely upon the automatic guidance provided by the tracks to steer in the right direction, the Type 157 did require some light input from the driver, who adjusted the steering gently based on the friction noises coming from the tyres and the wheel flanges.

The Type 157, during both tests and operations, had much to recommend it. The vehicle could reach and hold its top speed of 80km/h, and the braking properties proved very positive, with little skidding on wet or dry rails. Yet having been developed by the spring of 1944, by this stage of the war the strategic situation and the pressures upon German war production meant that few of the vehicles entered use, and the type remained relatively obscure.

However, although the number of variants listed on websites can number in the dozens, in many cases these vehicles remained mostly experimental, interesting concepts that never made it beyond a few prototypes. Research by Jochen Vollert for his recommended book, *Kübelwagen on all Frontlines*, lists three major types beyond the standard troop carrier version: the Type 821 *Funkwagen* (Radio Car), the Type 821 *Nachrichtenwagen* (Signals Car) and the Type 821 *Instandsetzungswagen* (Workshop Car), plus 273 Type 82 Kfz. 3 *leichter Messtruppkraftwagen* (Light Ranging Car). The first two vehicles on this list (3,326 and 7,545 produced respectively) were communications vehicles, fitted with radio equipment in the rear seating area. The Workshop Car (2,324 produced) included a removable work bench, welding equipment and a comprehensive set of tools in the rear compartment and in a locker behind the driver's seat, while the *leichter Messtruppkraftwagen* featured equipment for range-finding enemy artillery (Vollert, pp. 11–12).

The Kübelwagen was immensely popular and

the modest production of the VW factory never kept up with demand.

The Schwimmwagen

On 5 July 1940, Porsche received yet another approach from the HWA. With Hitler's operational gaze turned both west towards the UK and east towards the Soviet Union, the Wehrmacht was interested in an amphibious vehicle, based on the Type 87. Like the Kübelwagen, the new vehicle had to be light, nimble and durable, and suited to the exigencies of mass production under war conditions. It was envisaged that the amphibious vehicle would have particular utility in reconnaissance roles, the ability to cross rivers meaning that it could get to places prohibited to conventional vehicles. Ferry Porsche, Ferdinand's mechanically capable son, took charge of the project, and the Porsche Design Bureau set out to create what was in effect an amphibious version of the Kübelwagen.

The first iteration of what would become known as the Schwimmwagen was the Type 128. Following the Porsche Design Bureau's commission, it took just over two months to produce three prototype vehicles, all of which utilised a full-length Kübelwagen chassis with a 2,400mm (94.5in) wheelbase. To achieve the amphibious capability, the car's bodywork was

ABOVE A high-quality restoration of a wartime Type 166 Schwimmwagen. This photograph shows to good effect the front profile of the amphibious hull. *(Author's collection)*

RIGHT The pressed-steel hulls of Schwimmwagens, seen here on the production line at the Berlin-based Ambi-Budd company. *(Courtesy of the Volkswagen Museum)*

transformed by leading Porsche designer Erwin Komenda, who created a welded pressed-steel bodytub, with cross-member reinforcing to provide rigidity. This bodytub had boat-like contours and a smooth underside, to ensure the most efficient movement through the water – in effect, it was a powered hull fitted with

wheels. (Given that the vehicle floated extremely low in the water, any measure that could reduce the volume of wash was essential.) The vehicle was devoid of doors to avoid sealing problems. To deliver propulsion in the water, it was installed with a three-blade propeller mounted on an A-frame which hinged up on

RIGHT The Trippel amphibian was one of the Type 166's main competitors, although it was slower and less manoeuvrable than the VW vehicle. *(Courtesy Oliver Barnham)*

to the rear deck. When the vehicle was in the water, the propeller was hinged downwards into the water, engaging with a coupling from a crankshaft extension to provide power.

In good going, the Type 128 Schwimmwagen could maintain a decent 10km/h (6.2mph) across the water. Ingeniously, the Schwimmwagen also retained its front wheels for steering (it had no rudder), which meant that the driver could still use the steering wheel to guide himself through the water. Out of the water, the Type 128 relied upon four-wheel drive and self-locking ZF differentials to power it cross-country.

Testing of the Type 128 prototype began on 1 November 1940, and it was pitted against competing vehicles over 3,500km (2,175 miles) of road and off-road terrain, plus a total of 18 hours on the water. The results were promising. It outperformed its rivals on fuel consumption, amphibious capability and also cross-country resilience, and this success led to the HWA commissioning a further 100 vehicles at the beginning of 1941, with bodywork built by the Drauz company.

Testing of the Type 128 continued throughout much of 1941, with a particular focus on mountain trials and amphibious challenges. Time and again the Type 128 did not disappoint. Taylor Blaine, in his book *Volkswagen Military Vehicles of the Third Reich*, proves this point via a quotation from an official German Army report following some 2,580km (1,603 miles) of mountain tests:

Driving mountain paths in the high mountains under difficult conditions, as at the Kitzbühler Horn [where Ferry Porsche was present] or at the Rudnecker Alm near Watsching, sometimes muddy, rocky, very narrow and steep, demonstrated to us as never before the Type 128's extraordinary off-road capability when driven sensibly. We drove on paths that had never before seen a motor vehicle, and the total weight always amounted to almost half a ton. The vehicle's water capability did not fall short after its great off-road test runs, as it performed faultlessly in rivers at a higher speed than that of the other vehicle.

(Blaine, 2004, p. 98)

SCHWIMMWAGEN REPORT

The following text is from an article entitled 'German Light Amphibious Car', published in the US Military Intelligence Service's *Intelligence Bulletin* in December 1944:

The German light amphibious car, which resembles a small civilian sports car and has a boat-shaped open body, is highly maneuverable. The Germans call this vehicle a Schwimmwagen, literally enough, while on the Allied side it sometimes is spoken of as an amphibious Volkswagen. The light amphibious car represents a development of the original Volkswagen ('Peoples Car'), a light civilian vehicle that Hitler once promised to manufacture in huge quantities and bragged about as one of the future blessings of German National Socialism.

The light amphibious car has the following dimensions:

Over-all length (with propulsion unit in land-travel position)	11ft. 8in.
Over-all width	4ft. 10in.
Over-all height (with top up)	5ft. 2in.
Tread width, center line to center line	4ft.
Wheel base	6ft 6in.
Ground clearance (unloaded)	11.5in.
Approx. depth of immersion when floating	2ft. 6in.
Freeboard (loaded)	1ft 1in.

The following details have been obtained from a manufacturers plate in the engine compartment of a car examined recently:

Type	166
Payload	958lb.
Weight empty	2,002lb.
Permissible axle load (front)	1,190lb.
Permissible axle load (rear)	1,775lb.
Permissible total weight	2,965lb.
Engine capacity	1,131cc.

This specimen was fitted with "run-flat" tires, size 7.85 by 16.

(US Military Intelligence Service, 1944)

ABOVE August 1942. Three Schwimmwagens operated by the *SS-Leibstandarte Adolf Hitler* Division lead a German parade through the streets of Paris. *(BArch)*

So far so good for the Type 128. Yet in early 1942 the vehicle was discontinued in favour of an improved variant, the Type 166. Although the Type 128 had delivered praiseworthy trial results, it was still felt that off-road manoeuvrability could be improved, plus the vehicle could be rationalised somewhat for ease of production. Thus the Type 166 had reduced dimensions – its wheelbase was 400mm (15.7in) shorter (which improved its turning circle and lowered its weight) and its overall width was dropped

by 100mm (3.9in). More testing of the new vehicle was conducted, and this began in March 1942 with reservoir trials. Further tests took place in July on the Grossglockner Mountain, Austria, to see if the Type 166 could handle both steep terrain and snow (which it could), then followed more amphibious ordeals on the Ammersee in Bavaria.

Despite their seemingly endless propensity for testing, the HWA finally gave the green light to full production of the Type 166 in the autumn of 1942. The vehicles' major mechanical components were manufactured for the next two years at the Volkswagen factory at Fallersleben/Wolfsburg and the Porsche plant in Stuttgart, while the bodies were made by Ambi-Budd in Berlin. The vehicles started arriving on the front lines with army and Waffen-SS units in the autumn of 1942.

The Type 166 Schwimmwagen has the accolade of being history's most mass-produced amphibious vehicle. In total, during a tumultuous period in Germany's history, some 14,283 were produced, most of them at the Fallersleben/Wolfsburg plant. As we shall see later in this book, they were put to good use, whether ferrying boxes of ammunition across a Russian river swollen by the spring thaw, or powering reconnaissance units around the forests of the Ardennes in 1944. Yet in mid-1944 production ceased, as the noose of impending defeat began to close around Germany's neck. Material shortages and constraints on production facilities caused by Allied bombing meant that Germany was

BELOW The top-mounted exhaust pipe of the Type 166 Schwimmwagen, with the propeller deployment handle clipped to the top and a machine-gun mount to the rear. *(Author's collection)*

progressively forced to rationalise and prioritise its industrial products. The Type 166 had a clear purpose when Germany was on the offensive, particularly in reconnaissance roles. As the war closed in and pushed through Germany's borders, however, such a vehicle became an unnecessary indulgence, like many other weapons and vehicles in Hitler's arsenal.

Post-war life

At the end of the Second World War, with Germany virtually a ruin, hundreds of thousands of ex-military vehicles either rusted where they sat, were scavenged for metals or components, or were put to hard use resurrecting post-war economies and societies. Vehicles that had little post-war utility quickly disappeared, and the Schwimmwagen was no exception. In today's thriving market for Second World War military vehicles, the Type 128 and Type 166 remain worldwide rarities, especially the Type 128, of which there are only single-digit survivors, compared to several hundred Type 166s. Most of these, furthermore, have required huge restoration work to return them to an authentic appearance or working condition.

The picture with the Kübelwagen is different, not least because of the volume in which they were produced. In the aftermath of the war, thousands of the vehicles were put to continued use by opportunistic civilians in Germany and

parts, many were simply scrapped, but others sat untended in outbuildings and fields, waiting to be rediscovered and restored by future generations. Hundreds of Kübelwagens are therefore still to be seen at militaria fairs and vehicle conventions, as well as running in private hands around the world.

Yet the Kübelwagen not only survived in the continuing endurance of wartime vehicles. Such are the virtues of the Kübelwagen design, it was virtually inevitable that the car would be revisited and revised. A notable landmark was the development, in the mid-1960s, of the VW Type 181.

Type 181

in the many territories occupied by Germany during the war. The Kübelwagen's off-road characteristics and durability meant that they were ideal vehicles for light agricultural use, or for civilians living and working in less-developed regions. When they finally ground to a halt, typically on account of the lack of

During the 1960s, European powers attempted to integrate themselves increasingly through military standardisation, as part of the interoperability ambitions sought through the North Atlantic Treaty Organization (NATO), and also as part of the attempt to find economies of scale in the production of military equipment. One of the European multinational projects was the Europa Jeep, the intention being to design and mass manufacture an amphibious four-wheel-drive light utility vehicle similar to the American Jeep. The

Europeans began the bureaucratically tortuous development programme in the 1960s, but it quickly became clear that the new vehicle would not be produced overnight. In fact, the programme would never reach a significant fruition, and was cancelled in 1979. In the interim, therefore, the German government requested that VW build a suitable vehicle unilaterally, to fulfil immediate requirements for the fledgling Bundeswehr.

Although VW had rejected a similar proposal in the 1950s, in the 1960s there was a greater incentive – military and commercial. Not only was there the potential of sales within Germany, but there was an emerging civilian market around the world. This was the era of the dune buggy – light recreational vehicles capable of tackling off-road terrain for leisure pursuits. Mexico was one country expressing an interest in VW's activity, and the United States also offered a large potential market.

Rather than work from scratch, VW had a good starting point in the Kübelwagen, to which they imported thinking from other vehicles, such as the Type 1 Beetle, the Type 1 Karmann Ghia, the VW Microbus and the VW Transporter. The result was a vehicle that was transparently related to the Kübelwagen. It had the same air-cooled rear-engine layout, a convertible hood and the corrugated bodywork panels followed similar angles and lines, although with a deeper front storage area. The spare wheel had now been moved from the top of the scuttle to under the bonnet. It was also generally larger – the wheelbase was 2,400mm (94.5in), overall width 1,641mm (64.6in) and overall height 1,621mm (63.8in), with a ground clearance of 201mm (7.9in) at maximum payload. In the military version, the vehicle was still utilitarian in feel, but greater luxury came with the civilian versions. The seats were from a VW saloon, there was an electrical socket, and (in the 411 version) even a gas heater that ran directly off the car's fuel supply, meaning that the owner could heat the car without turning the engine on.

The Type 181 sold across Europe, the United States and Mexico during the 1970s, with manufacture taking place in Wolfsburg and Hannover (1968–74), Puebla, Mexico (1970–80), and even Jakarta, Indonesia (1973–80). It took a variety of evocative appellations,

including 'The Thing' (United States), 'Safari' (Mexico), 'Pescaccia' (Italy), 'Trekker' (United Kingdom) and 'Kurierwagen' (West Germany). In terms of its 'unique selling points', a VW advertisement in the United States spelled out the benefits:

A car ready to take on almost anything ...

Ready to take the bumps, the lumps, the rocks and the ruts. It's got a high ground clearance. A platform frame that shields the underparts from flying stones and debris. A four-wheel-drive independent suspension so that each wheel takes bumps separately. And a double-jointed rear axle that makes the rear wheels hug the ground. It's a car built tough, but it isn't tough to drive. For a small car, it's a heavyweight.

A car that goes just about anywhere ... on the beach, dune buggy style. Take the doors off, take the windows out, fold the windscreen down, fold the backseats down (and load up your gear), lower the top and let the sunshine in. If it rains, don't worry. Water drains out. Seats dry out without mildewing. And to help you get in and out of the dunes, its air-cooled engine is mounted over the drive wheels for better traction. Leave it to Volkswagen to help you make a good thing even better.

(Volkswagen of America, 1973)

ABOVE A rear view of the Type 181, otherwise known as 'The Thing'. The engine was a 1,584cc four-cylinder type generating 46hp at 4,000rpm. *(via Wikimedia Commons)*

The Type 181 sold in respectable quantities worldwide, although it was struggling against increasing competition from new types of lifestyle vehicle. Military sales to Germany were solid, however – some 50,000 vehicles were supplied to NATO between 1968 and 1979. At the end of this period, the German authorities began to make the switch to the VW Type 183 Iltis.

VW Country Buggy

A reflection upon the post-war evolution of the Kübelwagen would be incomplete without a brief survey of the VW Country Buggy, an adaptation of the Type 1 that again reconnected with the Kübelwagen in layout and concept. The Country Buggy (or Type 197) was a specifically Australian creation. Looking to provide an outdoor vehicle suitable for both work and play in Australia's tough outback and its rugged coastlines, VW Australia began development work in 1967. Existing VW components were put to good use – the Type 1 engine, gearbox and front axle were married to the rear reduction axles from the VW Transporter, these raising

the ride height and also serving to improve the vehicle's traction. The layout was also classic VW, with a rear-mounted 1,285cc four-cylinder air-cooled engine generating 50bhp. The chassis had a tubular centre section frame with a welded-on platform, plus independent torsion bar suspension. Atop the chassis was a pressed-steel body minus doors, with a fold-down windscreen. For weather protection there was the option of either a removable vinyl fibre canopy or a fibreglass hardtop with removable side curtains.

The Country Buggy, as it was called when it went into production in 1967, had enough of the Kübelwagen ancestry behind it to be recognisably part of the family. Interestingly, there was possibly also a nod back to the Schwimmwagen. … The prime movers behind the vehicle, VW Australia Engineering Manager Cyril Harcourt and Quality Control Director Rudi Herzmer, originally intended that foam sections should be implanted in the body panels, to give the vehicle an amphibious capability. This idea, however, was quashed centrally by VW in Germany, and Wolfsburg issued a series of

directives before it would give approval for production. These included the requirement that the new vehicle use as many existing Australian components as possible and that production could not interfere with other VW manufacturing goals. Output was to be limited to 1,800 units per year.

So in 1967 the Country Buggy went into production and on to the sales forecourts. VW Australia was blunt about the vehicle's attractions – the strapline of one of its press adverts read: 'If you think the Beetle is ugly … take a look at this one. VW Country Buggy. The uglier Volkswagen built for rugged dirty work.'

The Country Buggy was not a major commercial success, not helped by the fact that VW Australia's parent company was at this time essentially developing the Country Buggy's rival, the Type 181. Production was complete by 1969, with 1,956 built. Not all of those went into the domestic market. There were export sales to the Philippines, Singapore and New Zealand. Interestingly, the name for the Country Buggy in the Philippines was 'Sakbayan', a combination of the Tagalog words *sasakyan* (vehicle) and *bayan* (nation or people). The implication of this title was that

here was another 'People's Car', the Country Buggy resonating with history once again.

It should be noted that globally thousands of old VW Beetles were converted into 'Beach Buggies', simply by removing the old bodywork and substituting open-top, doorless fibreglass tops. These Beach Buggies were very popular, and had the advantage of being generally cheaper than buying a purpose-built vehicle.

Enthusiasts

Today, the Kübelwagen and the Schwimmwagen, as well as the post-war vehicles described above, are kept alive by a small army of vehicle enthusiasts worldwide, who hunt down, purchase and restore the ageing vehicles with commitment and often a meticulous eye for period detail. These individuals maintain not only landmark pieces of vehicular engineering, but also a time in which thousands of soldiers depended on such vehicles for their operations and survivability. The story of the Kübelwagen and Schwimmwagen is therefore as much about the people who used them as it is about the vehicles' technology.

BELOW The large radio aerial extending from this German Army Kübelwagen on the Eastern Front indicates that it is serving as either a radio car or signals car. *(Nik Cornish at www.stavka.org.uk)*

Chapter Two

Basic design and features

The Kübelwagen and Schwimmwagen are triumphs of rational engineering. Everything superfluous is stripped out, while everything of actual value is retained, producing functional and dependable military vehicles, tried and tested in both war and peace.

OPPOSITE The front headlamp incorporated a 6V 35W main bulb and a 1.5W side light. Undoing the screw at the bottom of the fitting allowed the user to remove the lens. *(Author's collection)*

29

The Kübelwagen is not a complicated vehicle. It is, however, an ingenious vehicle, using simple and logical design principles to achieve the structural properties and performance required for its military role. During the war, a US Ordnance School report gave a useful four-point summary of what it felt were the 'Salient features of the design':

1) *Good design on all important chassis components.*
2) *The use of the best materials where needed, with nonstrategic materials used on all non-essential items.*
3) *Fine steering balance and roadability obtained by having light unsprung weight and sensible distribution of weight.*
4) *Throughout the vehicle it is noticeable that lightness and simplicity have been the keynote. Simplicity has, in itself, brought lightness.*

The last sentence here, with admirable concision, sums up the central virtue of the Kübelwagen. In this chapter, we will look in more detail at the basic design and engineering proposition in both the Kübelwagen and the Schwimmwagen, noting how such simple vehicles were the products of an immense amount of considered thought.

Basic engine/ transmission layout

An especially useful source of mechanical information about the Kübelwagen, one that will be quoted extensively in this book, is the US War Department's TM E9-803, *German Volkswagen*, published in 1944. The publication is an extremely detailed study of the Kübelwagen in terms of layout, operation and maintenance, and was based on a vehicle captured in the North African theatre in late

BELOW The driving area of the Kübelwagen. Note the standard wooden slats that formed the vehicle's flooring. *(Author's collection)*

1943. As an English-language source for understanding the technical composition of wartime vehicles (not post-war restorations), the manual is rivalled only by the Humber report.

At the opening of its 'Description and Data' section, TM E9-803 gives a useful overview of the essential layout of the vehicle:

a. *General. The Volkswagen is a four-wheeled, rubber-tired, rear axle drive personnel carrier and reconnaissance car, comparable in purpose and size to the American ¼-ton 4x4 truck [the Jeep]. No propeller shaft, as such, is used; the engine, transmission, and differential comprise a unit structure which is secured to the floor at the extreme rear end of the vehicle. Access to the engine is provided by a hinged door at the rear of the body. The vehicle has no frame. Instead, a base stamping comprising the floor of the vehicle is ribbed and provided with a central tunnel to give desired stiffness, to form the foundation of the vehicle. The main fuel tank is located under the front body panel on the right-hand side of the vehicle. The spare tire is carried on top of the front body panel.*

b. *Engine. The engine is an air-cooled, four-cylinder, four-cycle, horizontally-opposed type. Intake and exhaust valves are located in the cylinder head and are operated by conventional rocker arms and push rods.*

c. *Transmission. The transmission is the selective, sliding-gear type. Four speeds forward and one reverse are available. Differing from American vehicles, no direct drive is used. The fourth speed forward is an overdrive, having a ratio of 0.80 to 1.*

(US War Department, 1944, p. 2)

Some aspects of this description need further comment. First, why the rear-engine layout? Obviously having an engine at the rear of the vehicle creates a rear weight bias, but in off-road vehicles this weight distribution actually improves traction, while also helping to avoid the non-power wheels digging into soft ground. Rear-wheel-drive cars also have better traction during acceleration and better weight transfer

during braking, when compared to front-wheel-drive vehicles. The downside is that a rear-wheel-drive car can have a tendency towards braking and lift-off oversteer, but the Kübelwagen compensated for that with its generally low speed and its limited slip differential, although depending on the load carried and its distribution the driver might have a lively time controlling the vehicle. (More about the actual driving experience of the Kübelwagen

ABOVE The spare wheel of both the Kübelwagen and the Schwimmwagen sat on the front of the vehicle, anchored to the mount by three screws. *(Author's collection)*

BELOW A view showing the front hull of the Schwimmwagen, featuring the tow point at the front and showing the front suspension support arms. *(Author's collection)*

is described in Chapter 5.) The location of the engine also facilitated a key ingredient of the Kübelwagen's rationale – an air-cooled engine. By having the engine at the rear, this actually had more efficient heat transfer from the engine into the atmosphere than if the engine was at the front.

In terms of the engine itself, the Kübelwagen is (as noted) of a four-cylinder type, the cylinders arranged in an 'H' shape in two horizontally opposed banks of dual cylinders. The cylinder heads are attached to the aluminium crankcase by long studs, and in the bottom of the crankcase is an oil sump, finned on the underside. The casing of the crankcase also provides a mount for various engine components, such as the dynamo and oil cooler. For the exhaust system, the engine has four exhaust manifolds leading from the cylinder heads; these pipes feed into two silencers located at the front of the engine on early models, while a silencer is located either side of the engine on later models. The engine gases vent out through two exhaust pipes. At the front end of the engine unit, the

gearbox is held into a recess in the chassis by a rubber donut. At the back end, the engine and gearbox are supported by a crescent-shaped cradle incorporating a rubber insert, the rubber fittings allowing a certain degree of rotational movement to absorb torque reactions from the motion of the vehicle.

The transmission and differential of the Kübelwagen are held within a magnesium base alloy cast-aluminium housing as a unit. The gearbox itself sits just in front of the rear axle, while the clutch is behind the axle. The gear-change rod runs through a centre steel tunnel (visibly running along the centre of the floor) and links up to the gearstick, which sits just to the right of the driver's seat.

The US manual clarifies the flow of the fuel from tank to engine:

Fuel for the Volkswagen is carried in an 8-gallon [40-litre] tank located under the right front cowling. The filler pipe for the tank projects through the cowling and is equipped with a snap-on cap. From the tank, fuel flows into a fuel strainer and sediment bowl mounted beneath the fuel tank; then is forced up through a wire mesh screen and into the flexible fuel line leading to the fuel pump, which is mounted on the engine. The fuel pump then forces the fuel into a fuel line to the carburetor which, in turn, introduces the fuel into the intake manifold. Air is drawn into the carburetor from a port in the left wall of the engine compartment. An oil-bath air cleaner removes dust from the air and conducts the air to the carburetor air intake. (US War Department, 1944, p. 81)

The carburettor is of a simple downdraught type, with a manually operated choke.

The air-cooling system on the Kübelwagen illustrates the continuing simplicity of the type. To maximise the cooling effect applied to the engine, a centrifugal fan blower is fitted, mounted in the generator armature. To give the blower access to the air, there are air inlets cut directly into the bodywork above the rear engine compartment, and these allow air to pass into the fan cowling through a 152mm (5.9in) hole; the air can then be blown through a baffle arrangement to circulate around the cylinders.

RIGHT The Schwimmwagen filler cap. The Schwimmwagen had two fuel tanks, set in front of the driver's compartment. *(Author's collection)*

RIGHT The Kübelwagen had a fuel cock set beneath the dashboard, just ahead of the front passenger seat, to provide i) fuel flow, ii) reserve supply and iii) fuel shut-off. *(Author's collection)*

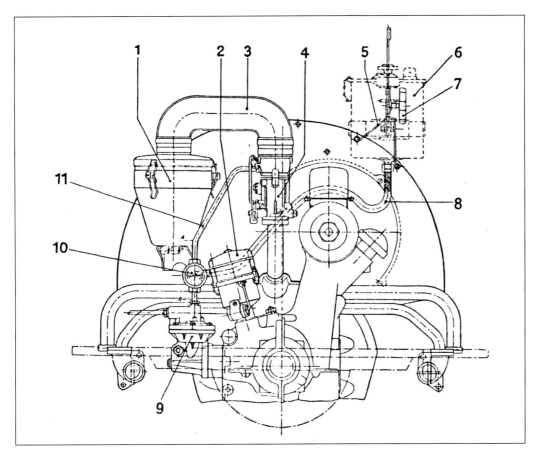

LEFT The Kübelwagen engine.

1. Air filter.
2. Distributor.
3. Induction pipe.
4. Carburettor.
5. Cold start petrol tank housing.
6. Cold start petrol tank.
7. Adjusting screw.
8. Flexible fuel pipe.
9. Fuel pump.
10. Two-way valve.
11. Fuel pipe.

On VW 82s made for tropical conditions, a cowl was fitted over the rear air intake so that air was drawn into the engine's oil bath air filter from inside the vehicle. The vehicle hood thus acted as a primary filter to remove many of the sand particles before the air was drawn into the main filter.

Suspension and shock absorbers

The Kübelwagen's torsion bar suspension is one of its noteworthy features, as it makes a signal contribution to the vehicle's off-road capabilities. Looking at the rear of the vehicle, each wheel has independent suspension, as detailed in the British Humber report, noted in the introduction:

It consists of torsion bars situated transversely in front of the rear axle and enclosed in a tubular cross member forming part of the underframe. Longitudinally swinging arms are attached to the outer ends, which have a trailing action. In turn, these carry the outer ends of the swinging

half-axle casings to which they are rigidly connected. The suspension linkage for each wheel thus represents two sides of a right-angled triangle, the wheel being situated at the right-angled corner. Consequently the wheels oscillate about an axis formed by the hypotenuse of a triangle. …

(BIOS, 1946, p. 32).

The report goes on to note that the essential value of this type of suspension is its simplicity: 'It entails only one universal driving joint per half-

LEFT The Kübelwagen's rear tow hook. A PaK anti-tank gun towing variant of the Kübelwagen was developed, but appears never to have entered production or service. (Author's collection)

ABOVE **A diagram from the US War Department manual on the Kübelwagen, showing the front suspension removed.** *(US War Department)*

BELOW **An exploded view of the Kübelwagen's front suspension, showing the ends of the flat torsion bars inside their housings.** *(Crown Copyright)*

BOTTOM **The front suspension with the torque rods removed.** *(US War Department))*

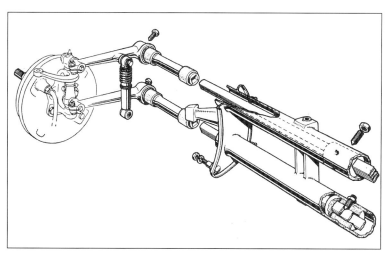

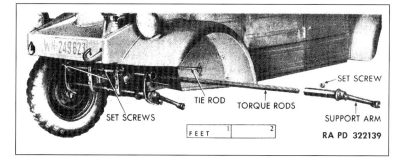

axle and the longitudinal arm which serves the dual purpose of the torsion bar suspension arm and the brake torque arm.'

Moving to the front of the car, we also find independently sprung wheels working on a torsion bar system, although of slightly different design to the rear wheels.

The front axle consists of two rigidly attached tubes bolted to the body frame forward of the tunnel housing. The support arms are anchored within the axle tubes and are free to pivot. The torque arm pins attach to the support arm, and support the kingpin bearings. The front wheel spindles are affixed to the vertical kingpins which pivot freely. The front wheels are independently sprung on torque rods within the axle tubes. The torque rods are four individual lengths of band steel and stretch along the entire length of the axle tubes. A nut and set screw at the middle of each rod have been set to counteract twisting and side-to-side movements, and to allocate shock to each side of the suspension. Shock is transmitted from the support arms to the torque rods. Stops, with rubber buffers, prevent excessively violent springing action and the single acting, hydraulic shock absorbers dampen the return swing.

(US War Department, 1944, p. 106)

The front suspension system has two primary virtues – it is both cheap and compact (as the Humber report observed) – although the efficiency compared to round bar suspension is considerably less.

As well as a difference between front and rear suspension in the Kübelwagen, there is also a difference between front and rear shock absorbers. At the front, the shock absorbers are single-acting telescopic affairs, which cushion the return spring action of the front torque rods. The rear shock absorbers, which also have to cope with the weight of the engine unit, are of a piston-operated double-acting hydraulic type. All told, the suspension and the shock absorbers worked together well to give the occupants if not a comfortable, then at least a tolerable journey over the roughest of terrain. However, the two front telescopic shock absorbers were not the strongest parts of the vehicle, and were subject to failure under heavy use. For this reason, on post-war VWs they were replaced by longer and stronger units.

Steering system

The Kübelwagen was known for its agility in steering, with even some impressed Allied observers noting that it could be thrown into corners with more aggression than a Jeep or equivalent British vehicle. The author of the US War Department report noted that the 'steering wheel and steering mechanism are of the conventional type commonly used in American vehicles'. The technicalities of this statement were expanded upon later:

The steering gear is the worm and sector type, and differs from the conventional construction in that the steering worm shaft is short, and an extension is used to connect the worm shaft to the steering wheel. The sector shaft is fitted with a socket into which the sector bearing is located. The sector bearing is designed to mesh with the threads of the worm shaft. The sector shaft extends through the steering gear housing, and the steering Pitman arm attaches to the lower end of the sector shaft. The opposite end of the Pitman arm is designed to accommodate two ball studs which are located in the inner ends of the tie rods. The tie rod ball studs are attached to the Pitman arm, and the tie rods extend to the steering knuckle arms. Ball studs in the outer ends of the tie rods are attached to the steering knuckle arms.
(US War Department, 1944, p. 117)

Brakes

The brakes on the Kübelwagen and Schwimmwagen work via a cable gear that is shared by both the footbrake and the handbrake, although these systems can still operate independently of one another. The brakes themselves are of fairly functional and economical design, being the two-shoe internal expanding type. The brake drums are integral to the wheel hubs, and 'Water-excluding means are provided by fitting a deflector cover, which is clipped on the outside of the back plate'

KÜBELWAGEN SPECIFICATIONS – FROM US WAR DEPARTMENT REPORT

a. Vehicle specifications

Vehicle specifications	Metric	Imperial (US)
Wheel base	2,400mm	7ft 10½in
Length, overall	3,740mm	12ft 3¼in
Width, overall	1,600mm	5ft 5in
Height, top down	1,111mm	3ft 8in
Tire size		5.25-16
Tire air pressure (front)	1.4 atm	20.5lb
Tire air pressure (rear)	1.8 atm	26.5lb
Tread (front)	1,356mm	53.39in
Tread (rear)	1,360mm	53.54in
Crew	4	
Weight (empty)	725kg	1,598lb
Weight (loaded)	1,160kg	2,557lb
Net load	450kg	992lb
Ground clearance	290mm	11.4in
Foot brake works on		4 wheels
Hand brakes work on		4 wheels
Wheels		Disc
Type of rims		Drop center
Front wheel toe-in	3–6mm	⅛–¼in
Camber		2½ deg
Caster		5 deg

b. Performance

Performance	Metric	US
Minimum speed	3kmph	1.8mph
Maximum speed	80kmph	49.7mph
Climbing ability in loose sand		40 pct
Climbing ability on the road		45 pct
Fording depth (without wetting engine)	450mm	17.7in
Operating radius	400–450km	250–280 miles

c. Capacities

Capacities	Metric	US
Main gas tank	40 litres	10.5 gal
Normal fuel consumption	8 litres/100km	30mpg
Transmission and differential		40 pct
– For lubrication change	2.5 litres	2.6qt
– For filling after overhaul	3.0 litres	3.1qt
Engine		
– For oil change	2.5 litres	2.6qt
– For filling after overhaul	3.0 litres	3.1qt
Steering mechanism	0.25 litres	½pt

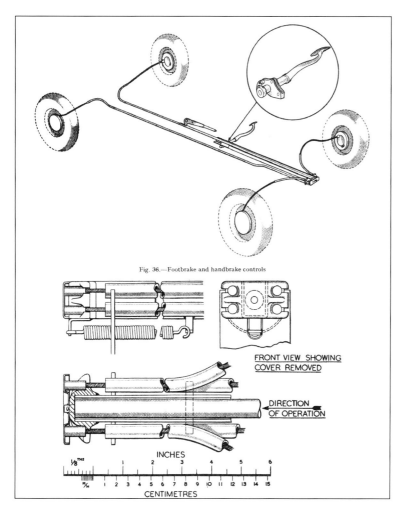

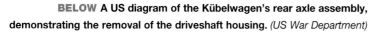

Fig. 36.—Footbrake and handbrake controls

FRONT VIEW SHOWING COVER REMOVED

DIRECTION OF OPERATION

ABOVE Another diagram from the BIOS/Humber report, this time showing the footbrake and handbrake controls, plus (at the bottom) the brake control head. *(Crown Copyright)*

RIGHT Extract from a German wartime 'Tropical Equipment Guide' illustrating some of the stages in changing a 'balloon' sand tyre. *(Courtesy of Oliver Barnham)*

BELOW A US diagram of the Kübelwagen's rear axle assembly, demonstrating the removal of the driveshaft housing. *(US War Department)*

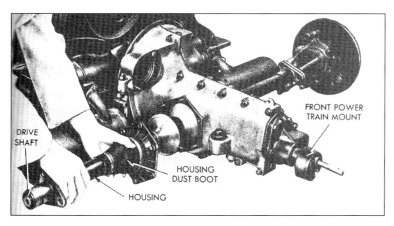

DRIVE SHAFT

HOUSING DUST BOOT

HOUSING

FRONT POWER TRAIN MOUNT

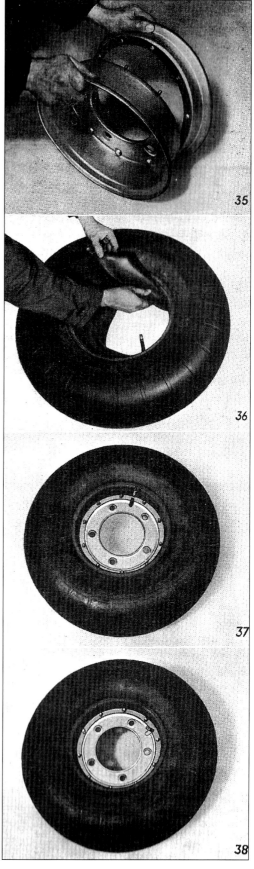

35

36

37

38

(BIOS, 1946, p. 45). When it is pressed, the footbrake applies braking to all four wheels, giving a well-controlled braking sensation. This pedal unit is in turn part of a single pedal-unit sub-assembly, which contains all the pedal controls and is bolted securely to the underframe backbone. The cables to the pedals are housed in rigid tubes and flexible conduits.

The handbrake, meanwhile, sits atop the underframe backbone. It is not a high-quality affair – the lever itself is simply a piece of folded steel hinged to a steel pin, with a standard ratchet and pawl engagement mechanism. Heavy-handed use by a muscular soldier could result in the handbrake being ripped up from its mount or the lever being stretched back to an unusable angle.

Tyres and wheels

Regarding the captured Kübelwagen's tyres, the US War Department noted: 'The Volkswagen is equipped with five steel disc wheels with deep set rims, and low-pressure synthetic tires and tubes, size 5.25-16. Air pressure should be approximately 20 pounds in front tires and 26 pounds in the rear tires' (US War Department, 1944, p. 121). Actually there was some variation in both rim and tyre types – the description here related to the standard rim and standard tyre. In addition, there was a special rim and corresponding tyre for desert conditions, known as the *Ballonsandreifen*. The sand tyre was larger (to give a more even distribution of ground pressure) and almost treadless, to give good traction on very sandy surfaces. Conversely, the standard tyre could be fitted with snow chains in sub-zero environments. It should be noted that some photos of Kübelwagens show various non-standard military and civilian tyres fitted. There was also a wide-profile tyre known as the *Kronprinzenrad 200-12*, which was frequently fitted to the Type 166. Hubcaps were issued for the VW 82, but generally these weren't worn in front-line service.

RIGHT The windscreen wipers were basic devices; the windscreen itself was a one-piece section made from shatterproof glass, which could fold forward and clamp to the cowl. *(Author's collection)*

Bodywork and windscreen

On riding in the Kübelwagen, you are struck by the rather flexible feel of the whole apparatus. The Kübelwagen had, as one of its overriding construction objectives, the need to keep the bodywork as light as possible, in turn to keep the operating weight of the vehicle to manageable levels.

The British Army, in their Handbook 87, provided a translation of the German D662/6 instruction manual for the Kübelwagen. Its description of the overall frame and bodywork is useful for familiarising ourselves with the layout of the Kübelwagen:

4. CHASSIS FRAME
The centre member is stamped out of sheet metal into semi elliptical shape, to the bottom of which a plate is welded, forming a 'tunnel'. It is forked at the rear to accommodate the engine and gear box. Towards the front it broadens to the frame head, which carries the front axle. The floor board plate is welded on. Through the backbone, in a welded bank of pipes, run the throttle control, air control, clutch and the two rear brake cables and tie-rod of the parking brake and the gear box remote control rod. The petrol piping is also in the backbone.
[...]
12. BODYWORK
The all-steel body has an equipment compartment over the front and rear axles,

body; to open the equipment compartment the back rest must be folded forward.
13. STOWAGE OF TOOLS AND ACCESSORIES
The petrol dip stick is in front of the right front seat and the first aid box on the left under the windscreen. On the left side panel at the front is the box for the inspection lamp and the driving documents. The compartment for the night march equipment and the driver's assault pack is in front of the vehicle, and the co-driver's assault pack is partly under the two front seats and partly under the right of the rear seat. The skid chains are under the rear seat, on the right, near the battery. The tools and jack are stowed in the engine compartment. The rifle clips are on the holding rod over the front seats and the shoes are on the floor plates. The shovel is secured in a sling to the right side panel and front mudguard.

(British Army, n.d., pp. 15–19)

The description is a useful one for an overall orientation to the Kübelwagen body, but there are details that can be added. For a start, the Kübelwagen bodywork and also component parts went through several iterations during the vehicle's production life. The rear of the vehicle, for example, was manufactured in four types, with variations in features such as the rear protection pan and a bar between the rear tow hooks for handling purposes. (These variations are explored in more detail in the photo captions.) Yet in general description, the steel of the Kübelwagen's tourer body was just 0.9mm (0.36in) in thickness, to achieve the requisite low body weight, so the ribbing was essential to give the vehicle some additional rigidity. The underframe was also of sheet steel, although of a thicker type. For the main floor, the steel plate was 1.2mm (0.48in), with a 2.48mm (0.098in) thick steel backbone running along the centre. At the front, the backbone supports the front torsion bar assembly; at the back it divides into two arms which hold the cradle for the engine and gearbox. The driver's foot pedal unit fits into the side of the backbone, and the handbrake lever is attached to the top.

and doors hinged to the centre pillar. The mudguards are bolted to the body. The windscreen is made of safety glass and folds forwards. Side curtains are provided, which can be stacked away in special compartments when not required. The front seats, with rigid back rests on the chassis, are adjustable. The rear seats are fitted in the

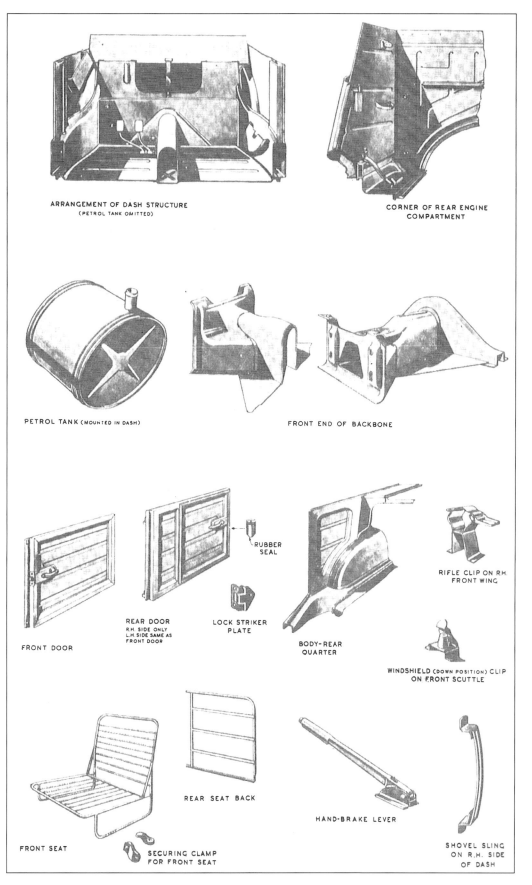

ARRANGEMENT OF DASH STRUCTURE
(PETROL TANK OMITTED)

CORNER OF REAR ENGINE
COMPARTMENT

PETROL TANK (MOUNTED IN DASH)

FRONT END OF BACKBONE

RUBBER
SEAL

FRONT DOOR

REAR DOOR
R.H. SIDE ONLY
L.H. SIDE SAME AS
FRONT DOOR

LOCK STRIKER
PLATE

BODY-REAR
QUARTER

RIFLE CLIP ON R.H.
FRONT WING

WINDSHIELD (DOWN POSITION) CLIP
ON FRONT SCUTTLE

FRONT SEAT

SECURING CLAMP
FOR FRONT SEAT

REAR SEAT BACK

HAND-BRAKE LEVER

SHOVEL SLING
ON R.H. SIDE
OF DASH

LEFT Details of
the Kübelwagen
bodywork, from the
BIOS/Humber report.
Note that these
illustrations relate to a
3-seat 'repair vehicle',
hence the extra
vertical rib in the rear
door and the seat back
for a single rear seat.
(Crown Copyright)

RIGHT The Kübelwagen could seat, at a push, three people in the back, although two was more customary. Note the rifle mounting bracket attached to the grab rail. *(Author's collection)*

Squirrelling down into construction details, the Humber report noted of its vehicle that:

The body structure is attached to the underframe by means of bolts, a continuous rubber insulating strip being employed between the two. The main outside joints are of the clinched flange type. Elsewhere spot-welding is employed throughout, reinforced with occasional gas-welding and rivets, where access is difficult for welding dies, or where additional strength is required.

(BIOS, 1946, p. 49)

BELOW A fine side-profile view of a restored Kübelwagen. The hole in the body just beneath the doors was an aperture for an insertable car jack. *(Author's collection)*

The total weight of the underframe and floor was 89kg (196lb), that figure including the foot pedals, gear lever, handbrake lever and tube for the rear torsion bars. The body frame was 229kg (504lb) in the Humber vehicle, including the 'wings, headlights (not side lights) [the main light shell actually incorporated the side lights as well as headlights], collapsible hood, windscreen, trafficators, floor (rear of "heelboard"), steering wheel and box' (BIOS, 1946, p. 52).

Above the floor, a wooden floor grating was fitted, held in place by the front seat brackets; this was useful for keeping the soldiers' boots out of any debris that collected in the floor wells. The doors on each side of the Kübelwagen hinged on the central pillar, and they could be easily removed by tapping out two door hinge bolts.

Looking in more detail at the car's superstructure, the Kübelwagen examined by Humber had three seats in total: driver and front seats, plus a single seat in the back on the left-hand side. (It should be noted that the Humber vehicle was actually a repair vehicle, with a tool locker in place of the right-hand rear seat.) The space by the side of the rear seat was used to accommodate a storage trunk. However, the Kübelwagen had a certain flexibility in its rear seating. It could either take a single full-width

back seat, accommodating three fairly slender people at a push, or it could be configured in a single-seat arrangement as described. Behind the rear seats was a general storage area, and the rear-seat backs could be folded down to provide more convenient access. The seats are all made of steel tubing fitted with rows of 'stretched' springs on which seat covers are attached.

The windscreen, as noted, was a folding affair, and when folded down it was held in place by spring clips on the scuttle. The scuttle was itself home to the vehicle's spare wheel, and there was a storage compartment beneath for the 20-litre (4.4 UK gallon) jerrycan. To keep the vehicle at maximum lightness, it did not have a rigid roof fitting, but rather a canvas hood featuring celluloid 'windows', the whole sheet stretched over a tubular-steel frame. The canvas hood had a single celluloid rear window. The hood fitted over a folding steel frame, and the Kübelwagen had side screens fitted with celluloid windows, which slotted into the four doors. This equipment gave weather protection greatly superior to that provided to the occupants of American MB/GPW Jeeps.

Electrical systems

The starting point of the Kübelwagen's electrical system was a 6-volt battery with a capacity of 75 ampere-hours, set under the rear seat on the left-hand side of the vehicle. This formed part of the vehicle's ignition system, which consisted of the battery, distributor, condenser, ignition coil, spark plugs and the associated wiring. (See Chapter 3 for more detail about the vehicle's ignition.)

The Kübelwagen's electrical fuses were housed in three boxes (later reduced to two), two sitting on the instrument panel fascia either side of the speedometer and one attached to the rear engine bulkhead. Each dashboard fuse box contained five fuses in total, and the user could identify which fuse related to which component by an explanatory card fitted to the inside of each fuse box cover. The left-hand box contained the following:

■ Horn.
■ Sidelight bulbs in both headlamps.

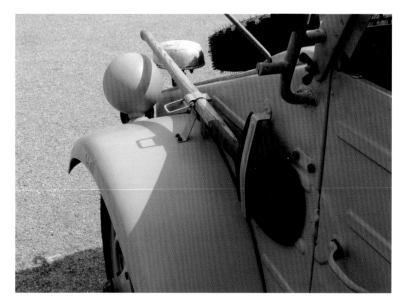

■ Dipped-beam filaments in both headlamps.
■ Main filament in left-hand headlamp.
■ Main filament in right-hand headlamp.

The right-hand fuse box contained the fuses for:

■ Notek blackout lamp.
■ Distance indicating lamp.
■ Trafficators and windscreen wipers.
■ Spot lamp.
■ Inspection lamp.

ABOVE From 1941 to 1944 the Kübelwagen had a spade mount on the left side of the body (earlier models had the mount on the right side). *(Author's collection)*

LEFT The Kübelwagen's direction indicators. On vehicles produced from late 1943 these indicators were attached directly to the windscreen side members, or simply omitted. *(Author's collection)*

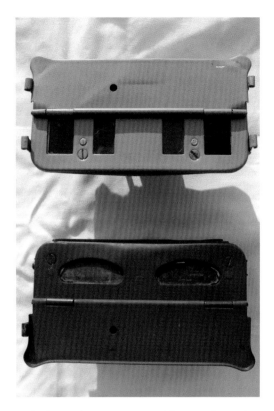

In the engine-compartment box on the early model Kübelwagen, there were three fuses in total: left-hand tail lamp, right-hand tail lamp and stop lamp.

Lighting

Much thought had gone into the Kübelwagen's lighting. Lighting on military vehicles is not simply a matter of throwing bright beams on to a road – extra issues such as concealment in hostile areas, off-road illumination and convoy distance holding have to be taken into consideration.

The Kübelwagen's total illumination package consisted of five specific lamps. Two of those were the mudguard-mounted headlamps, which had a total glass diameter of 170mm (6.8in), set in front of an aluminium reflector. Each lamp held two bulbs: a main bulb (6-watt, 35-filament) and a pilot bulb (6-volt, 3-watt), the former throwing out about 475 candlepower and the latter about 300 candlepower.

A Notek blackout driving headlamp sat on the front left-hand side of the scuttle. This light gave out minimal illumination in a narrow, downward-facing beam, to reduce the likelihood of the vehicle being spotted by enemy ground troops or passing aircraft. The length of the light's cowl was 105mm (4.2in), and the lamp glass consisted of fluted glass. Mounted on a swivel bracket on the body frame of early models, just to the right of the front passenger seat, was a Hella spotlight, for illuminating specific targets at distance. With a glass diameter of 110mm (4.4in), the lamp had a brass body and a switch at the back for operation. For discreet use, the lamp also had a rubberised canvas cover that could be stretched over the body and the glass, leaving a light slot of 2.5 × 0.5cm (1in × 0.25in) in the centre.

The most ingenious lighting device on the Kübelwagen was the rear Notek – a combined distance-indicating lamp and stop lamp, set on the left-hand rear. This lamp was fitted to all vehicles, military and civilian, in wartime Germany, except motorcycles. Essentially the lamp consisted of a die-cast or pressed-steel body, divided into two along the middle of its face by a hinged metal flap. In the upper half of the body was the distance-indicator part of the lamp, which had four vertical window slots arranged in separated pairs, with the two outer slots being larger than the two inner slots – 2.2 × 3.2cm for the larger two, and 1.8 × 3cm for the smaller two.

When the slots emitted light courtesy of a vertically mounted bulb behind them, the optical interaction of the lights with one another provided guidance as to the distance between the Kübelwagen and the vehicle behind it. The principle involved here is outlined with clarity in the Humber report:

The underlying principle of the distance indicator is the dependence of the resolving

power of the eye on the apparent angle of any object. The four windows indicate two limit distances.

1 The fusion of the two pairs of windows.
2 The fusion of all four windows.

Taking the average angular distance for the resolving power of one degree, these two distance limits will be 50 metres and 140 metres respectively. The difference in the sizes of the outer and inner windows enables the observer to estimate intermediate distances according to the extent to which the smaller window merges with the larger.

(BIOS, 1946, p. 62)

Roughly speaking, when the vehicles were following in convoy with one another through potential combat areas in which keeping distance was a tactical necessity, if the driver behind the Kübelwagen could see all four lights individually, rather than two blocks of two lights, he was too close.

Apart from the lighting system, electrical equipment was thereafter fairly limited on the Kübelwagen. There was a simple electric horn and also two windscreen wipers to keep the windscreen clean when it was in its flipped-up position.

Heating

By lifting a lever in the engine compartment, hot air could be directed from the engine fan housing through the body side panels to the inside of the vehicle.

Schwimmwagen amphibious system

The Schwimmwagen followed the same fundamental design principles of the Kübelwagen – a rear-mounted air-cooled engine; similar electrical layout above the waterline; commonality in many of the driving controls. The big difference, however, was

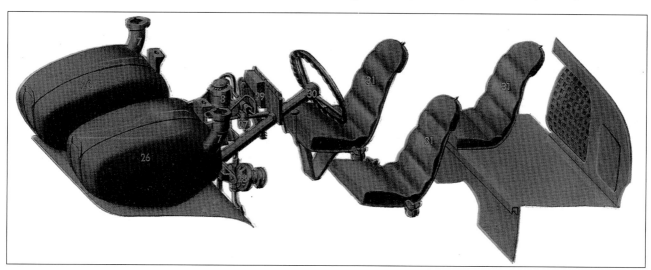

RIGHT The three-bladed Schwimmwagen propeller in its housing, with the hook aperture seen on the left. *(Author's collection)*

that the Schwimmwagen had amphibious capabilities, which required a waterproof hull, watertight protection for many key parts, plus a propulsion and steering system to keep it carving its way through the water in a meaningful direction.

Although a crude glance suggests that the Schwimmwagen was largely a Kübelwagen with its doors welded up, in fact the Schwimmwagen body shape was a highly sophisticated and aquatically efficient design. The US War Engineering Board noted this in a report in August 1945:

RIGHT Another image from D699/41, this time showing how neatly the engine and front axle fit inside the watertight hull unit. *(D699/41)*

In the impression of the committee the body or hull of this vehicle creates the impression of a well-engineered product. It is composed of a minimum number of stampings of substantial size, calling for an elaborate and expensive tooling program. The entire vehicle

would be costly to build from our standard for small vehicles. However, cost in a military vehicle is secondary to the man hours required in manufacture.

Efficient shaping of the body panels has resulted in a job having unusual roominess and a pleasant appearance. It has also contributed to light weight, structural stability and seaworthiness.

The shortness of the hull and the fact that the bow is fully rounded contributed to the success of front-wheel steering in the water, which is in contrast with standard boat-building practice.

(US War Engineering Board, 1945, p. 6)

High praise indeed. The Schwimmwagen was an intelligent design purpose-built for effective amphibious use, hence it is more accurate to talk about the vehicle's 'hull' rather than its bodywork.

The actual composition of the hull was explained in detail in a Wehrmacht user guide to the vehicle (D662/13), which explains the structure of the vehicle as follows:

The pressed steel body of the vehicle is similar in shape to that of a flat-bottomed boat.

Its main elements include a floor pan, two side members and front and rear sections. These parts are welded together and made watertight. The engine and accessories,

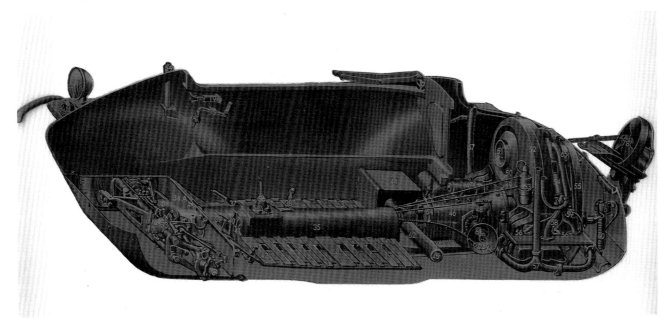

gearbox and rear axle drive unit are situated within the body. The steering mechanism, front suspension and front-wheel drive assembly are situated outside the hull and are individually waterproofed.

The strength of the hull lies in its curved form and two internal bulkheads, to which transverse and longitudinal stiffeners have been added.

A reinforced transmission tunnel which acts as a chassis frame runs along the floor of the vehicle, and carries the engine and gearbox at its rear end.

The front suspension and the differential housing incorporating the drive to the front wheels is bolted as a single assembly to the front of the transmission tunnel, with a rubber gasket sandwiched between the two elements. The gearbox control rods and a bank of pipes carrying the choke cable, throttle cable, clutch cable and rear brake cables, are located further down the tunnel.

(Wehrmacht, 1942, p. 28)

The reference to the Schwimmwagen as a 'flat-bottomed boat' is relevant here. For the Schwimmwagen is a true amphibious vehicle, designed from the outset to deliver as respectable a performance on water as it would do on land. The aqua-dynamic smoothness of the hull underside even led to the idea that the Schwimmwagen could double as a type of snow buggy, the sleek underbelly simply gliding across the snow while the wheels provided the power.

Unlike the Kübelwagen, the Schwimmwagen had a body with its joints welded over. Waterproofing was a natural issue for the Schwimmwagen. Ineffective waterproofing and protective lubrication would quickly lead to a

vehicle plagued by rust and parts malfunctions, so it was carefully designed to protect important components from water damage. Here the wartime German Schwimmwagen manual explains the waterproofing systems built into the vehicle:

b) Waterproofing

The joint between the front axle assembly and the open end of the transmission tunnel is sealed with a rubber gasket, which is compressed when the axle assembly and the hull are bolted together. In the floor at the front of the vehicle is a socket that carries the speedometer drive shaft, and this incorporates a rubber seal which is protected against damage by a metal cap.

The central lubricated feed-pipe to the externally mounted distributor valves is waterproofed by a rubber seal, which is screwed tight to the hull.

There is a slot in the front bodywork for the steering column, and this is sealed by a rubber ring which is gripped by a sheet-metal flange. The steering column itself is exposed to the water.

The two rear shock-absorbers are attached to the inside of the hull. Their operating shafts, on which arms are mounted, protrude outside. The shaft openings are sealed by conical rubber rings which, when the shock absorbers are bolted up, are pressed close to the body.

The rear axles are waterproofed as follows: The rear halfshaft tubes on each side of the vehicle leave the hull through spacious tunnels, each of which is provided with a flexible seal. These main seals take the form of large rubber boots, wide at one end and narrow at the other, and held in

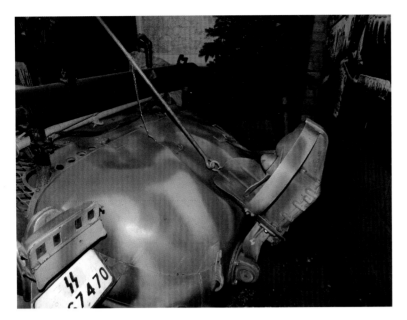

Backing up the Schwimmwagen's attention to waterproofing was a highly effective total-loss central lubrication system, designed to pump oil into key moving parts and displace any lingering water content. The heart of the system was a 1-litre (0.2 imp. gallon) oil reservoir connected to a hand-operated pump. The driver operated the hand lever several times, which pumped oil from the reservoir through a ball valve into a chamber, and then out through feed-lines to a distributor on each side of the upper torsion bar tube of the front suspension. From the distributors, the oil was then piped to the following points:

- The ball joints of the track rods.
- The plastic bearings on the torsion arms.
- King-pin pivots on the steering-knuckle housings.
- The pivot on the right-hand steering idler drop arm.

This oiling system ensured that the water content in important moving parts was pushed clear of the vehicle and not recirculated. The single-shot lubrication system was standard on many Wehrmacht vehicles, but was particularly suited to the Schwimmwagen.

Amphibious propulsion

Being watertight was one half of the Schwimmwagen's amphibious equation; its propulsion system was the other. This sat visibly at the rear of the vehicle's hull, in the form of a propeller on a hinged mount. The propeller was manually lowered by the operator, using a special rod, when amphibious propulsion was required. How the system worked is best described in the Schwimmwagen manual:

The propeller is mounted at the rear of the hull on a hinged 'A' frame assembly, which incorporates a chain drive in a waterproof housing driven from a power-take-off. When the frame is in the 'down' position, the propeller is engaged. The propeller is independent of the clutch and main gearbox, and is only capable of forward motion. Power is transmitted from the engine to the

ABOVE Here the Type 166 has its propeller unit in the upright position, with the operating rod engaged ready to lower the housing. *(Author's collection)*

place by adjustable metal straps. The wide end of each boot is connected to the rim of one of the two tunnel openings, the narrow end being attached to the adjacent output shaft cover on the gearbox. Thus water is prevented from entering the hull. To stop water from penetrating the gearbox itself, smaller rubber boots are attached to the inner ends of the axle tubes and these are also attached to the output shaft covers on the gearbox, the end fitting underneath the slightly wider ends of the other boots. The rubber boots are of heavy duty construction, reinforced and vulcanised for strength.

The power take-off unit for the propeller assembly is waterproofed with a gasket under its mounting plate. No special precautions are taken to prevent water from reaching the torsion bars and rods.

(Wehrmacht, 1942, p. 29)

RIGHT The Schwimmwagen propeller housing in its lowered position, the dog clutch engaged to provide power from the engine. *(Author's collection)*

propeller assembly through a flexible rubber coupling disc and a short transmission shaft to the power-take-off unit, which is held to the rear of the vehicle by a plate. When the A-frame is down, a dog on the propeller drive assembly mates with a similar dog on the power-take-off and forms an engaged clutch, which conveys power from the engine to the propeller. Securing this clutch is not necessary as when the propeller is in operation, water pressure forces the two dogs tightly together. Inside the propeller-drive housing a chain transmits power from the upper to the lower shaft on which the propeller is mounted. The lower propeller shaft incorporates a friction clutch that slips when necessary to give protection from

sudden shocks (for example, if the propeller is struck by a floating object).

[…]

A skeg is incorporated between the bottom of the propeller housing and the ring-guard to protect the propeller. If, when moving in water, the skeg encounters an obstacle, it will give way, causing the whole propeller assembly to rise up and uncouple. Once the obstacle is passed the assembly springs back into place and automatically reconnects. The swivel shaft has plastic bearings and requires no lubrication. The coupling and uncoupling action of the propeller can only take place when the gearbox is in neutral. Whenever there is a loss of power owing to the lifting of the

ABOVE This diagram clearly shows how the propeller unit took power from the engine; note the engaged dog clutch (108) and the chain drive running down from the driveshaft to the propeller itself. (D 699/41)

LEFT A close-up of the Schwimmwagen propeller dog clutch. Note that the clutch did not lock positively, but was held in place by a tension spring and by the water pressure created from the propeller. *(Author's collection)*

CENTRE Another view of the propeller dog clutch, seen through the mounting plate next to the tensioning unit, which kept the propeller either up or down. *(Author's collection))*

propeller, the driver must immediately slow down to enable the assembly to reconnect.
(Wehrmacht, 1942, p. 37)

The propeller system described here, like so much on the Kübelwagen and the Schwimmwagen, shows admirable ingenuity through simplicity. The dog clutch assembly was robust and reliable, while mechanical safeties meant that the mechanism could handle the inevitable and regular knocks from waterborne objects.

Note that the Schwimmwagen had no form of rudder to guide it through the water. Steering on both land and water came directly from the Schwimmwagen's front wheels. The driver would steer the car as normal on the water, with the directional force applied via the tyre treads taking the vehicle in the intended direction. Regarding the rims and tyres, the Schwimmwagen would take standard 5.25–16 cross-country tyres, but also 200–12 low-profile tyres for better performance across very soft or challenging terrain.

All told, the Kübelwagen and Schwimmwagen were triumphs of engineering, despite their modest appearance and lightweight construction. Much thought and consideration had gone into developing the vehicles for practical combat use. German engineering had, at times, a tendency towards over-sophistication and VWs replaced much

LEFT The Schwimmwagen horn, mounted higher up on the body to avoid damage during amphibious crossings. *(Author's collection)*

RIGHT The Kübelwagen had snap-on canvas curtains fitted with celluloid windows to give basic wet-weather protection. *(Author's collection)*

more sophisticated (and expensive) vehicles. It is unlikely, for example, that a tank such as the Soviet T-34 could ever have rolled out of German factories, although German engineers did take some inspiration from that armoured vehicle. With the Kübelwagen and Schwimmwagen, however, Porsche and his design team strove for and achieved durable simplicity, although we must not underestimate the sweat and intelligence that went into realising such principles.

TYPE 166 SCHWIMMWAGEN SPECIFICATIONS

Engine	1,130cc air-cooled, 4-stroke, 4-cylinder generating 25hp at 3,000rpm
Suspension	Rear: two adjustable torque rods Front: two torsion bars
Wheelbase	2,000mm (78.7in)
Wheels	Standard type: pressed disc with drop centre, 3.00 D/16
Tyres	Standard: 5.25–16 Low-profile: 20.0–12
Length	3,825mm (150.5in)
Width	1,480mm (58.3in)
Height (including canvas top)	1,615mm (63.6in) unloaded
Weight	Bare vehicle weight: 890kg (1,958lb) Unloaded weight (on road): 910kg (2,002lb) Max. permissible loaded: 1,345kg (2,595lb)
Axle loading	Front: 540kg (1,188lb) Rear: 805kg (1,771lb)
Ground clearance (loaded)	240mm (9.4in)
Turning circle	9m (29.5ft)
Draught (fully loaded)	770mm (30.3in)
Freeboard (at fully loaded road weight)	350mm (13.7in)
Speed at 3,300rpm	Low-ratio cross-country gear: 10km/h (6mph) 1st gear: 17km/h (10.5mph) 2nd gear: 32km/h (20mph) 3rd gear: 50km/h (31mph) 4th gear: 80km/h (50mph) Reverse gear: 9km/h (5.6mph) Max speed: 80km/h (50mph) Cruising speed in still water: 10km/h (6mph)
Highest possible gradient (max torque at 2,000rpm in low-ratio four-wheel-drive	Approx. 65%
Fuel consumption	8.5 litres (1.9 imp. gallon) to 100km (62 miles)
Fuel capacity	Left tank: 24 litres (5.3 imp. gallons) Right tank: 26 litres (5.7 imp. gallons)

Chapter Three

The engine and transmission

──●────────────

The beating heart of the Kübelwagen and Schwimmwagen was the air-cooled four-cylinder engine. It was not especially powerful, but allied to the light body of the vehicle it delivered all the performance required by front-line units.

OPPOSITE **This Kübelwagen engine has a** *Wirbelluftfilter* **air filter, a swirl-type filter introduced from 1943 and distinguished by its inverted-U profile.** *(Author's collection)*

51

THE ENGINE AND TRANSMISSION

RIGHT A rear view of the Type 166 engine, showing (foreground) the belt running between the camshaft pulley and the generator drive pulley. Note that the carburettor and distributor are from a post-war VW Beetle engine. *(Author's collection)*

BELOW The top half of the Schwimmwagen engine. Note the small fuel primer valve on top of the air inlet manifold; this could be used to introduce fuel straight into the carburettor if there were problems starting the engine. *(Author's collection)*

The Kübelwagen engine, described in outline in Chapter 2, was one of the triumphs of the car's engineering. With proper use and diligent servicing, it ran reliably across theatres ranging from the sand-blown North African deserts to the snow-choked wildernesses of the Soviet winter. This environmental reliability came from several angles – general build quality; the advantages of the air-cooled system; ease of maintainability – and it is doubtless the case that the Kübelwagen could operate where other vehicles struggled to do so.

In this chapter we will unpack the engine and transmission in more detail. Once again, we can draw upon the manuals and reports created during the war years, which give a direct insight into the engines as they were built and run. Note that many of the descriptions of the Kübelwagen engine apply equally to the Schwimmwagen; key differences will be noted.

Crankcase and crankshaft

The Kübelwagen crankcase was a two-piece aluminium alloy casting, with the joint located on the centre lines of the main bearings and the camshaft bearing. As an integral part of the casting, the crankcase also contained the oil sump, which the Humber report noted was 'of fairly wide and shallow proportions so as to afford maximum ground clearance'. For oil cleaning purposes, the sump was fitted with a detachable gauze filter/strainer. Furthermore, the underside of the sump had fins to aid oil cooling.

The Kübelwagen's crankshaft was made of a steel forging, 'hardened and ground on all bearing surfaces, and supported on four main bearings. Oil ways are drilled for pressure feed lubrication from the main journal to the connecting rod big end bearings' (BIOS, 1946,

p. 18). The connecting rods themselves have an H-section for structural rigidity, aided by the fact that they are quite short compared to many other vehicles of the time.

Pistons, camshaft and cylinders

The Kübelwagen engine had flat-head aluminium alloy pistons, with two compression rings and one scraper ring set on the top end. Detachable cylinder heads were also made from aluminium alloy.

A recess encloses the valve gear, and the whole casting is generously finned. The valves are arranged in line (disposed horizontally), two valves being fitted for each cylinder. The two inlet valves are situated in the centre and in consequence the inlet ports are interconnected in the cylinder head casting. Seating inserts are of bronze and are either pressed or shrunk in position and retained by peening over the surrounding metal; the valve guides are of phosphor bronze. Steel inserts for the sparking plugs are fitted and these are screwed up to a flange formed on the inserts and pegged in position to prevent them from working loose.
(BIOS, 1946, p. 19)

Each cylinder had two valves, with identical exhaust and inlet valves and interchangeable valve springs.

The rocker arms fulcrum direct on to hardened and ground shafts, an oilway being drilled from the push rod spherical seating to the rocker shaft. Adjustment for setting valve clearance is provided by a pin screwed into the rocker arm and operating the valve. Push rods operate the valve gear and these are unusual in their design, being in effect composite tappets and rods; the tappet ends of the push rods are guided (as a bearing) in reamed holes in the crankcase.
(BIOS, 1946, pp. 19–20)

Controlling the valves, the camshaft had four cams, with each cam operating two push rods and the associated valves. Three bearings

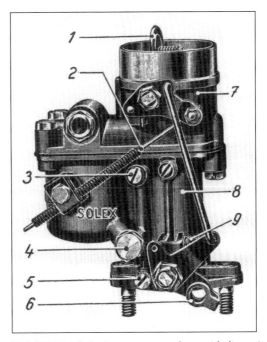

LEFT The carburettor on the Kübelwagen was a simple downdraught type, with no acceleration pump.

1 Choke flap.
2 Return spring for choke.
3 Idle jet.
4 Jet holder.
5 Volume control.
6 Throttle lever.
7 Upper body and float chamber.
8 Throttle body.
9 Throttle stop.

BELOW The Schwimmwagen engine, set in its watertight compartment. *(Author's collection)*

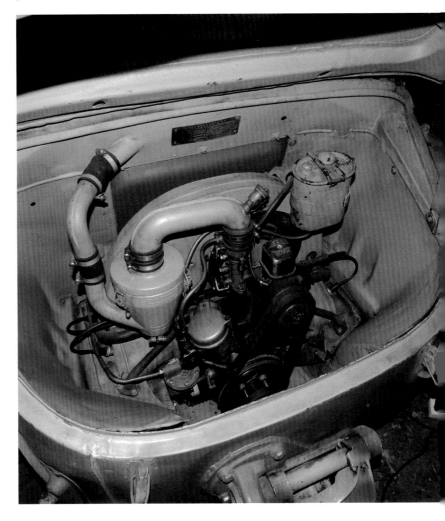

ABOVE Detail of the engine fitted to a Schwimmwagen, showing fuel pump with tap on top to the auxiliary 'cold start' fuel tank (top right). *(Author's collection)*

BELOW A diagram showing the main lubrication points on the Kübelwagen engine. *(US War Department)*

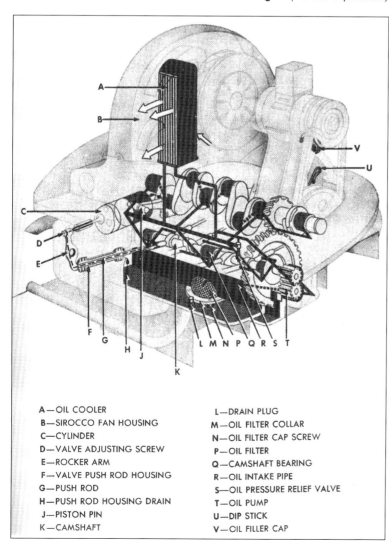

A—OIL COOLER	L—DRAIN PLUG
B—SIROCCO FAN HOUSING	M—OIL FILTER COLLAR
C—CYLINDER	N—OIL FILTER CAP SCREW
D—VALVE ADJUSTING SCREW	P—OIL FILTER
E—ROCKER ARM	Q—CAMSHAFT BEARING
F—VALVE PUSH ROD HOUSING	R—OIL INTAKE PIPE
G—PUSH ROD	S—OIL PRESSURE RELIEF VALVE
H—PUSH ROD HOUSING DRAIN	T—OIL PUMP
J—PISTON PIN	U—DIP STICK
K—CAMSHAFT	V—OIL FILLER CAP

supported the whole structure. At one end of the camshaft is a flange that attaches to the gear drive, and there is also a slot for connecting with a tongue on the oil pump spindle.

Lubrication

The core elements of the Kübelwagen's oil system are the crankcase sump, oil pump and oil cooler. The sump has already been noted, but the US War Department report explains it in more detail:

The oil strainer assembly is built into the bottom of the engine crankcase and consists of a strainer, cover plate, two gaskets, six nuts, and six lock washers. The oil strainer is shaped like an inverted cup with an open end cylindrical depression in the center to accommodate the oil flow tube. Oil is drawn through this oil flow tube by the pump, and is distributed throughout the engine. The engine does not have the conventional oil pan, but the bottom of the crankcase is finned for oil cooling purposes. The oil strainer assembly is mounted to six studs by lock washers and hex nuts and may be easily removed for cleaning.

(US War Department, 1944, p. 77)

As the quotation explains, the oil is pulled through the strainer – a gauze filter – into the oil pump, located at the rear end of the crankcase. This pump, as described above, is powered by the camshaft, and it drives the oil through drilled holes in the crankcase on to the crankshaft, camshaft and push-rod bearings. The oil is also pushed through the push rods to the rocker-arm bearings, and drains back down to the oil sump through the push-rod tubes.

Highly visible, and mounted on the left side of the engine block, is a tall, tower-like oil-cooler system, which comprises a series of vertical tubes and fits within the fan housing. At the base of the cooler is an inlet tube and an outlet tube, both sealed against the unit with rubber seals or grommets. The inlet and outlet tubes allow the vehicle's oil to flow into the main system, once it has been cooled.

As mentioned in Chapter 2, the Schwimmwagen was fitted with a central

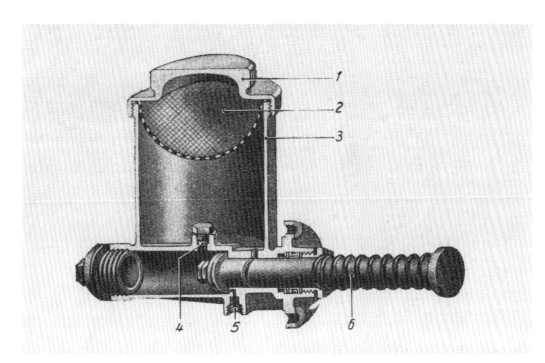

lubrication system which was manually operated. It was designed as a total-loss system – after an amphibious action, the operator would pump a handle several times to force oil to key moving parts, driving out any lingering water.

Air cooling and cleaning

The advantage of air-cooled engines is that they can operate in both extreme heat and extreme cold with little modification. The basics of the air-cooling system are described in Chapter 2, but the most important element of the system is the air-circulating equipment, which the Humber report describes thus:

The air circulating equipment is particularly noteworthy, being totally enclosed in a metal cowling, air access being arranged at the rear through a 6 in. [152mm] dia. hole. Air is drawn through this orifice and into the cowling by means of a rotor, which is keyed to the dynamo armature shaft (at the opposite end to the drive), and runs at a speed 1.75 times that of the engine.

The rotor is a casting of magnesium alloy [pressed steel in late-war and post-war VWs], and has blades arranged for circulating air by centrifugal action. The oil cooler is enclosed by the cowling and

deflectors are arranged for distributing air to each bank of cylinders and the oil cooler. Provision for cooling the dynamo is also incorporated by arranging auxiliary blades on the rotor which draw air through the centre of the dynamo.

The cowling is formed in two halves from steel pressings, lap jointed on the periphery and spot welded together. It is held rigidly by a large magnesium alloy cast flange mounted on the dynamo, and has ducts arranged to enable air to flow through the dynamo into the atmosphere.

(BIOS, 1946, p. 21)

RIGHT The cold-weather kit was seen on both the Kübelwagen and Schwimmwagen. This small petrol tank held high-octane fuel to assist engine starting under extremely cold conditions. *(Author's collection)*

RIGHT The oil-bath air cleaner device centrifugally spun dust particles out to the side of the container, where they were trapped by oil. *(Author's collection)*

RIGHT A rare cross-country carburettor type fitted to the Kübelwagen. *(Author's collection)*

A concluding sentence at the end of this section notes that 'the operation of the air-cooling system is extremely noisy'. This is certainly true, although the noise levels dropped to more manageable levels as you moved closer to the front of the vehicle (i.e. it was better to be in the front seats than the rear seats), and when the vehicle was under way the fact that the engine was rear-mounted served to carry much of the noise away.

The Kübelwagen's carburettor was a basic downdraught type, consisting of a float chamber and combined float chamber and throttle tube, with a manual choke. Of this design, the US engineers noted: 'It is simple in design and, because its primary aim is economy of operation, no acceleration pump is used. The idle mixture adjustment and the throttle stop screw are the only external adjustments provided' (US War Department, 1944, p. 83).

Sitting next to the carburettor was an air cleaner, which needed to be very efficient if it was to handle the dust and debris of the battlefield while keeping the carburettor inlet valve fed with clean air. The air cleaner was an oil trap type (although late-war VWs were fitted with dry cylinder 'whirlwind' filters). Air entered the conical housing, which was fitted inside with a very fine wire filter cage, and was swirled around in a centrifugal action. This action threw the heavier dirt out of the walls of the filter, where the dirt was trapped by oil in the system. The Humber writers observed that 'Oil may be drawn with the air into the filter, but as the passages are very fine the restriction makes it practically impossible for any dust to pass through without being caught by the oil' (BIOS, 1946, p. 22).

Ignition system

The Kübelwagen's ignition system consisted of the battery, distributor, condenser, ignition coil, spark plugs and the associated wiring. The distributor was of the four-cylinder centrifugal type, with an automatic timing control. Allied investigations of the distributor found that the component's bearing did not have a direct method of being oiled, instead relying on surplus oil from the engine. Given that the bearings were made from cast iron, the conclusion was that these components were likely to give the vehicle trouble over time. To the author's knowledge, however, it is unclear whether this part was particularly prone to faults.

Looking at other parts in the ignition system, the ignition coil was a standard 6-volt unit, mounted on the front of the fan housing. The high-tension wiring that linked out from the distributor was of 7mm (0.28in) rubber-covered type, with Bakelite mouldings at each end of the lead housing the suppressor.

The US War Department report explored the starting system and the vehicle's generator/dynamo in detail:

a. *Starting System. The 6-volt starting system consists of the battery, battery cables and ground cables, the cranking motor solenoid, and the cranking motor. The starting system operates independently of all other electrical equipment and wiring of the vehicle. When the cranking motor button is depressed, it closes the circuit between the battery and the cranking motor solenoid.*

b. *Generating System.*

(1) *The function of the generating system is to maintain a fully charged battery under all normal operating conditions. The generating system consists of the generator, generator regulator, and ammeter warning light. The generator regulator controls the output of the generator according to the requirements of the battery. The ammeter warning light on the instrument panel should flash on under the following conditions:*

(a) *When the ignition switch is turned on.*

(b) *When electrical equipment and lights are operating but the motor is not running fast enough for the generator to overcome the discharge from the battery.*

(c) *When electrical equipment is being operated with the engine not running.*

(2) *The generator regulator contains three units, each performing a distinct and independent function. These three units of the regulator are known as the circuit breaker, the voltage regulator, and the current regulator. It is mounted on the top of the generator.*

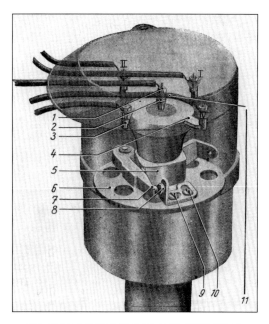

78. CRANKING MOTOR AND CRANKING MOTOR SOLENOID.

a. *Cranking Motor.*

(1) *DESCRIPTION. The 6-volt cranking motor is secured to the right-hand side of the transmission and differential housing. The cranking motor is equipped with a sliding gear which meshes with a ring gear on the flywheel to start the engine.*

[…]

The cranking motor solenoid is mounted on the cranking motor. The solenoid coil is energized when the cranking motor switch button on the instrument panel is pressed; the plunger in the solenoid is pulled toward the rear, which moves the

LEFT Distributor (ghost view) from the wartime Kübelwagen manual. *(Courtesy Oliver Barnham)*

1 Connector (HT current).
2 Carbon brush.
3 Contacts.
4 Rotor arm.
5 Cam.
6 Contact breaker plate.
7 Breaker arm.
8 Contact breaker point.
9 Lock screw.
10 Adjuster.
11 Suppressor.

LEFT The Bosch distributor, used on both the Kübelwagen and the Schwimmwagen engines, with the tall oil cooler system in the background. The cap on this distributor is post-war. *(Author's collection)*

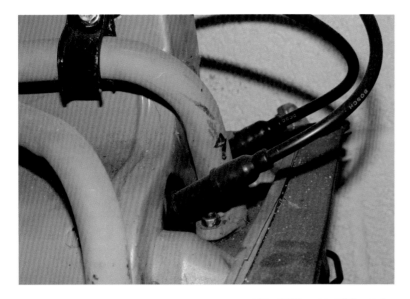

LEFT Spark plug leads and inlet manifolds on a Kübelwagen engine. *(Author's collection)*

CENTRE A close-up of the generator drive-pulley with the belt protected by an anti-splash cover – a standard fitment on Schwimmwagens. *(Author's collection)*

outer end of the cranking motor clutch operating lever. The cranking motor pinion is moved into mesh with the teeth on the flywheel to crank the engine.

[...]

79. GENERATOR REGULATOR.

a. Description. The generator regulator consists of three entirely independent units encased in a sealed, moistureproof and dirtproof box mounted on the generator. These units are: the circuit breaker, which closes and opens the circuit between the generator and battery to prevent the current from flowing back through the generator when the engine is stopped; the current-limiting regulator, which controls the maximum output of the generator and prevents damage to the generator and battery; and the voltage regulator, which holds the electrical system voltage constant within close limits under the various operating conditions.

80. GENERATOR.

a. Description. The generator is a 6-volt, two-brush unit mounted on top of the engine. It is driven by a V-type belt from the crank shaft. The output of the generator is controlled by the regulator which is mounted on top of the generator.

(US War Department, 1944, pp. 88–91)

In most environments and with good fuel, the Kübelwagen would start without too much coaxing, but in truly extreme cold-weather

LEFT A close-up view of an engine cylinder on an original Schwimmwagen engine. The cylinders were cast in one piece with integral cooling fins. *(Author's collection)*

conditions the engine needed an extra boost. For this reason, the Kübelwagen and Schwimmwagen were fitted with cold-weather starter kits. A small 1-litre (0.2 imp. gallon) fuel can was normally mounted on the top right-hand side of the fan housing and connected via a flexible pipe to the fuel pump. It was filled with high-octane petrol which, to avoid problematic engine starting, could be fed into the carburettor by turning a tap on top of the fuel pump. Once the engine was up and running without problems, then the winter kit could be turned off and the vehicle switched back to its normal fuel supply. This system was fitted to almost all Wehrmacht vehicles.

Gearbox

The Kübelwagen had a straightforward manual transmission, operated by a gearstick that pivoted in a pressed steel housing fitted atop the chassis backbone. The gearstick in turn was connected to the selector by a tubular control rod. The clutch, as observed by the Americans, 'is a single plate, dry disk type, and is installed in the engine flywheel. A bell-shaped housing, extending from the differential housing, covering both clutch and flywheel, bolts to the engine rear plate. The clutch release mechanism is incorporated in the clutch housing. No adjustment for wear is provided other than adjustments of the clutch pedal linkage' (US War Department, 1944, pp. 72–73).

Moving to the gearbox itself, the gearbox, clutch operating mechanism and the differential together comprised a single-unit structure, placed within a housing of magnesium base alloy and secured to the frame at three specific points: the front power train mount and the transmission and differential support arms. (Note that the gearbox also carried the starter motor.) The actual placement of the gearbox was in front of the rear axle.

The gearbox for the Kübelwagen had four forward speeds and a reverse, with the first gear being a 'crawler' gear to keep the vehicle at a constant walking pace alongside marching

BELOW A longitudinal cross section of the Kübelwagen's gearbox and clutch. The transmission and differential form a unit structure within a cast aluminium housing. *(Crown Copyright)*

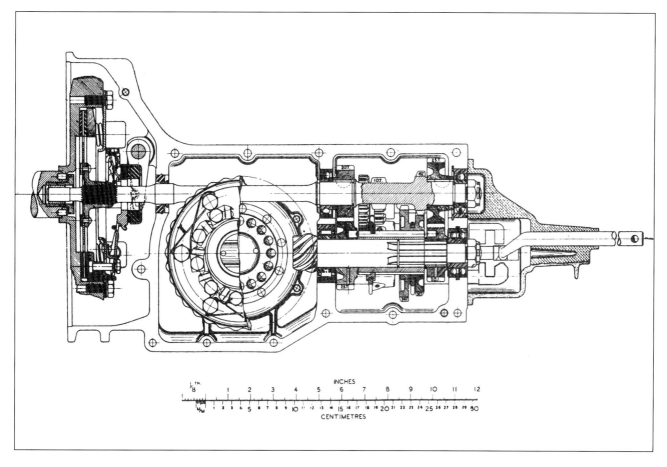

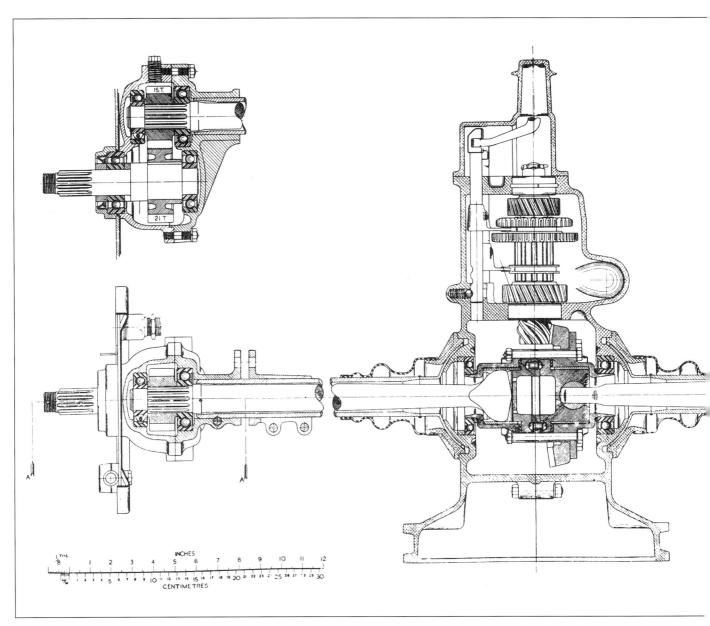

ABOVE **A cross-section of the Kübelwagen's rear axle and gearbox. The Schwimmwagen gearbox was very similar, except for the addition of a low ratio gear and power take-off for the front-wheel drive.** *(Crown Copyright)*

troops. (Note that under normal conditions, drivers start their Kübelwagens in second gear.) The transmission speeds and the respective gear ratio are as follows:

Transmission/speed ratio	
First	3.60:1
Second	2.06:1
Third	1.25:1
Fourth	0.80:1
Reverse	6.6:1

Both the Americans and the British had guarded praise for the Kübelwagen gearbox. For the Americans, the main point of note

was that the vehicle did not have the 'direct drive which is commonly used in American vehicles. This factor has been sacrificed in order to obtain compactness of design within the transmission and differential. Power is transmitted from the engine crankshaft to the flywheel, through the clutch to the transmission main drive shaft, which is splined to the clutch driven plate, and to the transmission driven shaft. A small pinion, called the rear axle driving gear, connects the transmission driven shaft to the large ring gear in the differential. This large ring gear turns the drive shafts which are connected to the final drive assembly in the rear wheels' (US War

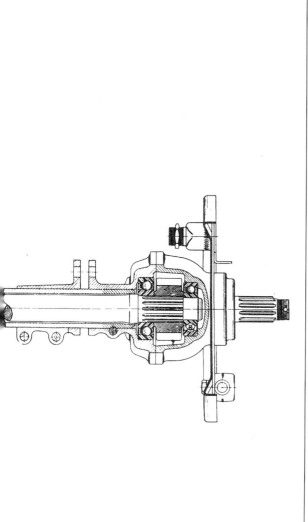

THE SCHWIMMWAGEN TRANSMISSION

The following passage is from Schwimmwagen manual D662/13, and describes the Type 166's gearbox in detail:

The gearbox incorporates a low-ratio 'cross-country' gear, a reverse gear, and four gears for normal road use of which the fourth gear acts as an overdrive. First, second and reverse are straight-cut spur gears. Third and fourth are helical-cut, and are engaged by long locking pins contained on the pinion-shaft in a sleeve which also carries first and second gear. The cross-country gear is engaged with a simple dog-clutch selector. The gearbox and the engine housing are bolted together, forming a single unit which is supported in three places on rubber mountings. The front end of the gearbox is enclosed in a rubber moulding located in an anchorage block that also secures the rear torsion rods. At the other end, the transmission sits on rubber pads in a crescent-shaped cradle, which is attached to the forks at the rear of the chassis frame by two bolts. The locating holes on the cradle are oversize to accommodate eccentric adjusters which are held in place by locking screws. By carefully turning these adjusters, the transmission cradle, and with it the whole engine and gearbox assembly, can be finely positioned around its centre point while being firmly held at the front end. In this way it is possible to precisely align the gearbox, crankshaft and transmission shaft to the propeller assembly.

(Wehrmacht, 1942, p. 23)

Department, 1944, pp. 99–100). The classic advantages of direct drive – for example, more efficient power output, reduced noise emissions, fewer moving parts (hence less servicing and a longer lifespan) – are, in the American view, passed over for the virtues of a compact vehicle, but there is the clear sense that the sacrifice is worth it.

For the British assessors, one of the key points of note about the gearbox was its method of gear engagement:

The gear engagement on the bevel pinion shaft provides a noteworthy feature. Nine pins fit in corresponding semi-circular grooves in the sleeve which is splined on to the shaft, and also in semi-circular grooves in the centre member. The pins act as the driving medium for the centre member, which gives either first or second speeds when in mesh. To obtain third or fourth speeds the pins are moved along the grooves by the selector and the ends engage with corresponding holes in one of the constant mesh gears. This design replaces the normal dog engagement and consequently reduces the overall length of the gearbox; it also provides easy engagement which is simple to produce.

(BIOS, 1946, p. 25)

LEFT The brilliant ZF limited slip differential, described below. *(Courtesy Oliver Barnham)*

1 Axle shaft, right.
2 Slides.
3 Cam disk, right.
4 Housing.
5 Crown wheel.
6 Bevel gear.
7 Guide lock.
8 Slipper disks.
9 Cam disk, left.
10 Sliding joint.
11 Axle shaft, left.

1   2   3   4   5   6   7   8   9   10   11

Differential

The differential on the Kübelwagen played a vital part in what made it such a success. The Kübelwagen did not have a particularly powerful engine, nor did it have the cross-country advantages offered by four-wheel drive (unlike the Schwimmwagen). Yet the differential was configured to ensure that the vehicle delivered excellent performance on even the roughest of surfaces.

The US War Department report summarised the differential system on the Kübelwagen as follows:

The differential is a positive locking type. It consists of opposed plates having a circle of indentations resembling small cams. One plate has nine of these cams and the other eight. Attached to the differential ring gear is a round plate with a series of holes in which small pawls, with rounded ends, slide back and forth in the irregular path provided by the above mentioned cams. This operation offers a differential action at slow speeds. However, if one plate carrying the cams begins to turn much faster than the other plate, which would happen in the event that one wheel was in mud while the other remained on dry ground, excessive friction would cause the pawls and the cams to lock, thereby transmitting torque equally to the two driving wheels.

(US War Department, 1944, p. 100)

BELOW An exploded view of the Kübelwagen clutch assembly. The Kübelwagen clutch was a single-plate, dry-disc type. *(US War Department)*

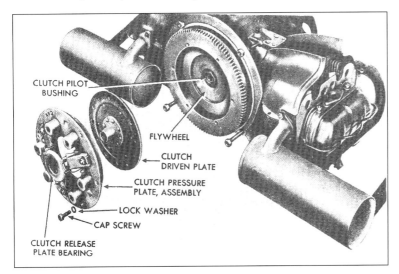

CLUTCH PILOT BUSHING

FLYWHEEL

CLUTCH DRIVEN PLATE

CLUTCH PRESSURE PLATE, ASSEMBLY

LOCK WASHER

CAP SCREW

CLUTCH RELEASE PLATE BEARING

The Kübelwagen's positive locking differential provided several performance advantages. It delivered excellent grip on soft ground, whether setting off or turning. Like any vehicle, the Kübelwagen could get bogged down in deep snow or thick mud, but as long as one of the drive wheels had contact with relatively solid earth it could generally find its way out of trouble.

Considered in the round, the Kübelwagen and the Schwimmwagen represented some of the best examples of German ingenuity in design. From the outset lightness, simplicity, functionality and low cost of production were key goals and Volkswagen replaced a wide variety of heavy, over-complicated field cars.

CROSS-COUNTRY VEHICLE DESIGN

Cross-country vehicles must meet many criteria to fulfil their role, some of them conflicting. For a start, the vehicle requires good ground clearance to protect the body from rocks and other obstacles. At the same time, however, by raising the ground clearance the vehicle designer must not heighten the vehicle's centre of gravity excessively, as this will make it unstable when rocking about over rough terrain or crossing gradients laterally. The vehicle's suspension has to be able to ride out the worst undulations of the surface without malfunction from impact or over-stress, while shielding the occupants from upward jolts and sudden drops. Since the off-road terrain can include mud and snow, generally the vehicle requires wide off-road tyres to distribute the vehicle's weight over a larger area. It should also have appropriate traction-control systems to get the power of the engine down to the ground, and compensate for wheelspin. The typical methods applied here are the locking differential, limited-slip differential and four-wheel drive.

BELOW A US diagram of the Kübelwagen engine. Note that the oil bath air filter shown here was later replaced by a dry *Wirbelluftfilter.* (US War Department)

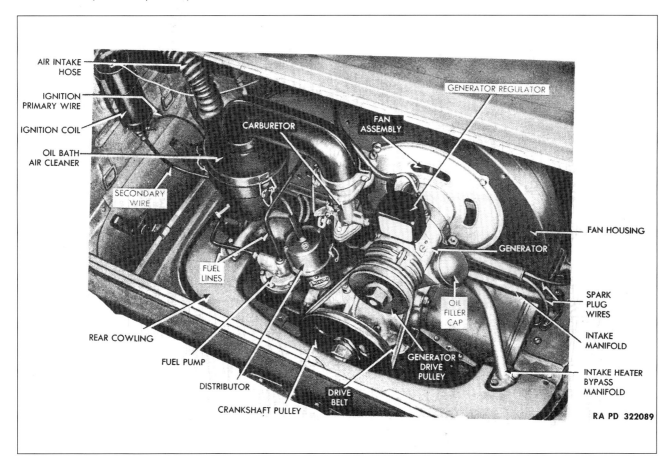

Chapter Four

In war and peace

The Kübelwagen and
Schwimmwagen were every
ounce operational vehicles.
What that meant was that every
mechanical component was
tested to destruction across the
Wehrmacht's theatres of war, with
thousands of men trusting their
lives to the vehicles in the most
dangerous places imaginable.

OPPOSITE A German Army Kübelwagen team in northern
France get their bearings, July/August 1944. Note how both
headlights are fitted with slit covers. *(BArch)*

Having acknowledged the engineering achievements of the Kübelwagen and Schwimmwagen, we must now answer a fundamental question – what did these vehicles actually do?

A glance through any photographic history of the Kübelwagen shows it cropping up in every corner of Hitler's temporarily expanded Reich. We see them grinding their way across the scorched roads and barren landscapes of North Africa as part of the Afrika Korps, their occupants baking in 40°C (104°F) heat. Conversely, on the Eastern Front the Kübelwagen and Schwimmwagen feature from the Baltic States to Stalingrad, showing how they kept pace with each advance and retreat. In that sweeping theatre, the vehicles wrestled with every environmental extreme: the hot dust and dense grasses of the Russian steppe in summer; the spring and autumnal *rasputitsa* (quagmire season), when heavy rainfall turned hardened tracks into depthless rivers of mud; the deep winter, with snow many feet deep and arctic-level sub-zero temperatures. The Kübelwagen and Schwimmwagen were also running through the lanes of Normandy and wider Europe following the Allied invasion of June 1944, the occupants nervously eyeing

ABOVE A Kübelwagen crew keep a careful lookout for enemy activity on the French roads, 1944. *(BArch)*

RIGHT Somewhere in Yugoslavia in 1943 or 1944, German troops take a break by the side of their Kübelwagen. A water crossing seems imminent, as one soldier wears a life jacket. *(BArch)*

the sky for fighter-bombers. They also served through Sicily, Italy and the Balkans, where they coped easily with the mountainous terrain.

What made these vehicles so highly prized in all these theatres? In a nutshell, they could operate where many other vehicles couldn't and, in a related advantage, they gave German forces a mobility around the battlefield that they otherwise wouldn't have enjoyed.

Reconnaissance vehicles

The photographic evidence shows that on countless occasions the Kübelwagen and Schwimmwagen were put to work as little more than light utility vehicles, filled to the brim with people, light weapons and crates of supplies. Yet neither vehicle was available in sufficient quantities to become a pure utility type; there were other wheeled and tracked vehicles that performed this role with greater heft and capacity. If we were therefore to define one major tactical role of the Kübelwagen and Schwimmwagen, it would be reconnaissance.

The Wehrmacht placed a high value upon powerful and flexible reconnaissance forces. By the outset of the Second World War in September 1939, the Heer (German Army) established mixed-vehicle armoured reconnaissance battalions within their Panzer and mechanised divisions, to provide optimal and occasionally aggressive reconnaissance

ahead of offensive spearheads. These units consisted of wheeled armoured cars, motorcycles (individual and with sidecar) plus a number of towed guns to give some anti-tank capability. Each Panzer division also had a full motorcycle battalion. Within the non-mechanised infantry divisions, reconnaissance support would come from a horse cavalry squadron, a motorcycle squadron, about three armoured cars plus whatever towed guns were available. Below the divisional level, motorcycle scout platoons provided the primary means for Panzer and motorised infantry regiments and battalions to conduct reconnaissance.

The advantage of the light, fast vehicles

ABOVE Afrika Korps troops move across the Libyan desert in 1941. A Kübelwagen is at the front; the highly visible swastika wheel cover acts as an identifier for friendly aircraft. *(BArch)*

BELOW North Africa, 1942. Here we see a Kübelwagen serving as a divisional command vehicle. *(BArch)*

was that they could be deployed with speed to advance positions such as key bridges and road-crossings. The armoured cars could clip along faster than the tracked tanks they were supporting. The forward positioning of reconnaissance units, however, often put them at the front line of the fighting, rather than conducting pure surveillance and observation. Indeed, as the war progressed, the line between reconnaissance probing and straightforward offensive action blurred considerably. Following the campaigns of 1939–40, this reality began to change the vehicular requirements of the German reconnaissance forces.

The changes gathered pace throughout 1941, as the German forces began to experience a very different style of warfare on the Eastern Front. Here, a long way from the familiarity of western Europe, the landscape, climate and distance proved to be far greater obstacles than the conditions in Belgium, France or the Netherlands. The motorcycle reconnaissance that had proved so useful in the West was exposed as having severe limitations in Belorussia, Russia and the Ukraine. Motorcycle riders, with nothing but a greatcoat between them and the elements, had limited battlefield endurance, and controlling the machines proved either exhausting or impossible across endless miles of thick snow or rutted tracks. If they found themselves plunged into fighting, furthermore, they were hideously exposed and had little in the way of personal firepower.

The solution was that between 1942 and 1943, the motorcycle component of German Panzer division reconnaissance forces was largely replaced by armoured cars and half-tracks, which offered much better survivability, but also by Kübelwagen and Schwimmwagen vehicles, which delivered enhanced mobility. In the motorised infantry/ Panzergrenadier divisions, the divisional armoured reconnaissance battalion had about nine armoured cars and instead of the SdKfz 250/251 half-tracks it opted for Kübelwagens. The Schwimmwagen was more extensively used by Waffen-SS units, who particularly appreciated the vehicle's capabilities for conducting amphibious reconnaissance across the Soviet Union's seemingly unlimited

LEFT Eastern Front, 1944. A Type 166 crosses a muddy plain in the company of what appear to be non-German cavalry forces. Note how the vehicle has snow chains fitted to the rear tyres to increase traction. (BArch)

waterways. (Like the German Army, the Waffen-SS also had reconnaissance battalions as an integral element of the division.) We should also note that large numbers of the Kübelwagen were also used by the Luftwaffe as reconnaissance, utility and staff cars.

The Kübelwagen and Schwimmwagen offered invaluable qualities as reconnaissance vehicles, particularly when compared to the motorcycles they replaced. (Note that motorcycle troops by no means disappeared from the German forces. Not only were individual riders used as messengers, but motorcycle and sidecar combinations, fitted with an MG34 or MG42 machine gun, were also used to deliver mobile firepower support for both infantry and armoured units.) Being protected from the elements, albeit to a rudimentary degree, the occupants of a Kübelwagen or Schwimmwagen could endure longer reconnaissance missions in adverse conditions. The performance of the vehicle in cross-country terrain was more tenacious, particularly in thick mud and snow, and driving a Kübelwagen avoided the physical threat of being thrown, a common experience of motorcycle troops. Another key advantage of the Kübelwagen and Schwimmwagen over motorcycle reconnaissance related to observation. When a motorcyclist was riding, especially off-road and in poor conditions, it was hard to do anything else except concentrate on the road or track immediately in front, let alone conduct reconnaissance

in transit. With the Kübelwagen, however, the driver could focus on keeping out of trouble while other occupants could conduct reconnaissance. The Kübelwagen could carry up to five personnel, depending on how the vehicle was configured, which meant that it could also park up in a camouflage position while its multiple occupants performed a broader squad reconnaissance. Finally, both the Kübelwagen and Schwimmwagen could carry heavier firepower than a motorcycle, meaning that it had greater fight-back in an armed encounter.

Of course, both the Kübelwagen and Schwimmwagen were applied to many other purposes. Although these vehicles had a limited capacity for carrying wounded soldiers,

BELOW Multiple Waffen-SS Schwimmwagen make an amphibious crossing on the Eastern Front, 1943. As the lead vehicle crawls up on to the bank, the man at the rear prepares to lift the propeller mechanism out of the water. (BArch)

the Kübelwagen, for example, had the mobility that could take it into the most difficult corners of the battlefield for casualty evacuation. Doctors and other medical staff routinely risked their lives in rescue attempts. For instance, during the early fighting in Normandy in June 1944, a Dr Roos of Fallschirmjäger Regiment 6 took his Kübelwagen forward to retrieve casualties from an American ambush around La Barquette. Despite moving out under the ostensible protection of the Red Cross, Dr Roos was ambushed on the way – men from his regiment found his body sprawled in the Kübelwagen near the church of St-Marie-Du-Mont.

The ability of the Kübelwagen to get into all corners of a battlefield meant that it was

highly regarded as a command car by the more aggressive breed of combat leader. To aid battlefield communications there was a three-seat radio car, the Type 821, which had the rear right-hand passenger seat replaced with tactical battlefield radio sets, for communicating with Panzer elements or with overhead Luftwaffe aircraft. German commanders also made frequent use of VWs.

Generalfeldmarschall Erwin Rommel, for example, often used the Kübelwagen to give him command mobility on the open battlefields of North Africa, enabling him to move quickly between front-line positions and units of the Deutsche Afrika Korps (DAK). Similarly, on the Eastern Front, Generalfeldmarschall Erich von Manstein had his own Kübelwagen. To maintain a good flow of communication between his headquarters and the various corps commanders, von Manstein would take his Kübelwagen alongside a radio vehicle, with an armoured car providing security. Even with the Kübelwagen delivering its off-road capability, life in the command car could still be hard – von Manstein noted that a journey of 30km (19 miles) on 2 September 1941 took him a grinding 8 hours and required his vehicle being pulled out of the mud by gun tractors on eight occasions. Even a Kübelwagen could get stuck!

What really made the Kübelwagen versatile were the purposes to which it was put by actual soldiers in the 'live' setting of an operational theatre. Here we see not only the exceptional

LEFT Travel through the snows of the Eastern Front was arduous in the extreme. The Schwimmwagen had no heating system. (BArch)

qualities of the vehicles, but also the equal quality of the vehicles' crews.

The Kübelwagen and Schwimmwagen in combat

The Kübelwagen's first foray into actions came in the Poland campaign of 1939, albeit in extremely limited numbers as pre-production vehicles. A reference to a Kübelwagen in this role comes from a German soldier, part of a reconnaissance battalion scouting out bridges and positions across the River Bug:

We had covered 50 kilometres [36 miles] getting to Ceichanoviec. It had taken us nearly as long to traverse the 15 kilometres [10 miles] of sandy desert. This is no good; we are losing valuable time. So we must get back to the main road. The scouts are re-directed. But the commander is too impatient to wait for this to be put into effect.

Then at the head of the column, which has just reached the main road, flares go up, and shots are fired. Darkness and peace then return. Shortly afterwards we hear from the leaders of the column that there are Polish troops of every kind, with many vehicles, on the move from north to south along the main road. At the same moment this news is confirmed in the strangest manner. The orderly officer of another reconnaissance detachment – accompanied by a light armoured reconnaissance car, a Kübelwagen and a motorcyclist – reports to our commander. He is rather pale. He had travelled for half an hour jammed into the middle of this Polish column. When he finally got to a side-road, he made himself scarce – and ran across our leading vehicles. You need luck in this world, especially soldiers.
(Guderian, 2011, n.p.)

It is interesting to note the composition of the reconnaissance unit, the light Kübelwagen being framed by the armoured car to provide greater security and firepower and the motorcycle for light tactical movement. (The author admits to the possibility that the Kübelwagen referred to here might not actually

BELOW Troops from the *Hitlerjugend* division are passed by a SdKfz 251D halftrack in France, 1944. The fact that the two central reinforcing beads on the doors extend past the tip of the door handle indicates that this vehicle was built after 1941. Note also the Panzer IV tank (right) with long-barrel 75mm gun. (BArch)

be a Type 82, as the term 'Kübelwagen' was applied to other vehicles of similar purpose.) But the true baptism of fire for the Kübelwagen was the North African campaign from 1941 to 1943. A very small number of these vehicles were present in the western Europe campaign of 1940, but the campaign was over before major deliveries of series-production vehicles began to reach front-line troops.

The experience of operating the Kübelwagen in combat in North Africa was an acid test for the vehicle's overall design proposition, particularly in terms of handling and engine reliability. As it turned out, the Kübelwagen performed admirably. Allowing for waxing hyperbole of propaganda, one German war correspondent painted a glowing picture of the vehicle in the desert war:

We rush past columns. The Volkswagen, air-cooled, small, tough, with sand-coloured paint, with the motor in the back, proves itself uniquely here and eats what the desert throws at it; it snorts, spits now and then, but handles everything, and we pat it on the back at night, as it deserves, and as everyone in Germany should know. Drive it where you will, my boy. Wipe the sand out of its neck and pipes so it feels your kind hand – it won't leave you in the lurch.

(Quoted in Piekalkiewicz, 2008, p. 49)

ABOVE The Kübelwagen could tackle gradients of up to 45%, depending on the terrain; here they move through battle-scarred territory in Yugoslavia. *(BArch)*

RIGHT A Kübelwagen demonstrates its speed and cornering ability on a baking-hot road in North Africa. *(BArch)*

A later report, published for internal consumption amongst Afrika Korps drivers, was much less bubbly in its expression, listing many pages of the problems facing Kübelwagen operators in desert conditions (see Chapters 5 and 6 for more details). However, nowhere in the report does the writer seem to suggest that the vehicle itself has fundamental design problems exposed by the desert – rather, the Kübelwagen comes across as a highly capable vehicle simply requiring more attentive maintenance and careful driving to get it to perform sustained operations in one of the harshest environments in the world.

One of the biggest combat threats to the Kübelwagen in North Africa, by late 1942, was the danger from Allied air attack. Eventually, the Allies achieved air superiority in all theatres, and that meant that Kübelwagen crews came to spend much of their time on the road craning their necks to the skies. In North Africa, travel across the sandy terrain tended to produce a dust trail that provided Allied aircraft with a clear vector of attack, so night-time travel might be required, depending on the level of threat. When the vehicles were parked near the front lines, tan camouflaged netting provided some measure of overhead cover, and in the flat landscape it was often necessary for the crews to dig in the vehicles up to door height, banking up the sand around the vehicle to provide a modicum of ballistic protection. Note that when the Germans had local air superiority, it was common practice to secure a swastika flag on the upper surface of their vehicles to identify them as German and thus protect them against 'friendly' air attack.

Of all the Kübelwagen and Schwimmwagen vehicles produced during the Second World War, the majority of them served on the Eastern

RIGHT The vehicle in North Africa here appears to be a Type 67, which consisted of a Type 60 chassis with a modified Type 82 body, adapted to carry two stretchers. *(BArch)*

of Belorussia; move ammunition and supplies amongst defensive positions; provide mobile communications around a rapidly changing front line and doubtless helped carry thousands of exhausted and wounded soldiers back to the Reich under the horrifying retreats of 1943–45. More about the actual driving conditions of the Eastern Front will be considered in Chapter 5.

The Kübelwagen and Schwimmwagen played their part in many other theatres. In both Italy and the Balkans their ability to negotiate the precipitous terrain that characterised the countryside was highly appreciated. In western Europe, following the D-Day invasion, both types of vehicle were used to zip rapidly around the front-line areas, whether transporting regular soldiers on reconnaissance or commanders wanting to get a detailed picture of the situation. There are several famous (and frequently miscaptioned) photographs of Schwimmwagen in use during the Ardennes Offensive with Waffen-SS formations. The classic image is meant to show SS-Obersturmbannführer Joachim Peiper, the leader of *Kampfgruppe Peiper*, 1 SS-Panzer-Division *Leibstandarte SS Adolf Hitler* (LSSAH), considering his route from a Schwimmwagen at a crossroads in the Ardennes. Actually, the officer shown was an SS-Unterscharführer from 2 Kompanie, Aufklärungs-Abteilung 1, and

ABOVE A Kübelwagen runs along the roads of southern Italy in 1943. The Kübelwagen proved itself extremely useful for negotiating the mountainous terrain further north in 1944. *(BArch)*

Front. A theatre of true total war, here the environmental conditions were seasonally far more extreme than in North Africa, and thus presented the vehicles and their crews with a whole different range of operational challenges. Certainly the vehicles were put to hard use: the Kübelwagen and Schwimmwagen were used to conduct reconnaissance for the major Panzer thrusts of 1941–43; transport troops on anti-partisan operations in the forests and marshes

RIGHT A Type 166 passes through a checkpoint in Italy in September 1943. The rear occupants have two Kar 98k rifles stowed at the ready. *(BArch)*

LEFT Another view of Schwimmwagen passing through the Italian checkpoint, this time accompanied by a Kübelwagen. The Kübelwagen has an intermediate-type rear body, featuring a broad protection pan underneath with two large access cut-outs. *(BArch)*

the photograph was staged by an authorised photographer, producing an undeniably evocative image. In fact, Peiper would not have even travelled along this route. What the photograph does capture, however, is the nimble mobility of the Schwimmwagen in difficult terrain. Its amphibious properties also facilitated movement across mud, snow and marshland – the smooth underbelly could glide across such surfaces, with the wheels providing the power.

Weapons fitment

In the vast majority of photographs taken of the Kübelwagen, no special weaponry is fitted to the vehicle itself. Certainly the interior is frequently seen well stocked with hand-held weapons. A rack was normally fitted to hold two or four Kar 98k rifles or, on occasion, Panzerfaust anti-tank missiles. The Kübelwagen could be upgraded to mount an

LEFT Two German paratroopers get a lift from a Kübelwagen in France, 1944. Note the heavy vegetation camouflage applied; Kübelwagen crews would often park under trees to avoid detection from the air. *(BArch)*

ABOVE Rifle racks for Kar 98k rifles in the back of a Kübelwagen; the large chest would hold machine-gun ammunition, amongst other war materials.

(Author's collection)

MG34 or MG42 machine gun when required, but these were rarely fitted. These special brackets could hold a machine gun pointing fore and aft. The front mount positioned the weapon conveniently for forward-facing use by the front passenger. This mount sat the weapon on a spring-balanced arm, giving it a rudimentary form of stabilisation for firing on the move. To the rear, the weapon could be fitted behind the back seat on a short pedestal mount, and was operated by one of the rear passengers. When the gun was not in use, it could be dismounted and locked into a bracket behind the front seats.

The two mounts described were primarily for ground fighting, but there are pictures of Kübelwagens with weapons configured for anti-aircraft use. These images are mainly seen on the Western Front from June 1944, as a response to the Allies' devastating air superiority. The standard multi-purpose MG34 mount for vehicles was the *Fliegerdrehstütze 36* pedestal, which was essentially the extension tube for the standard MG *Lafette* tripod mount but bolted to the floor and topped with the flexible *Dreibein* fork piece for mounting the gun. Also seen, however, are full *Dreibein 34* AA tripod mounts fixed within the rear passenger compartment. Given that such mounts occupy the space previously given to rear seats, this configuration would require the machine-gunner to be dismounted to operate

RIGHT This sketch of a Schwimmwagen shows the location of weapons and ammunition magazines. *(Courtesy Oliver Barnham)*

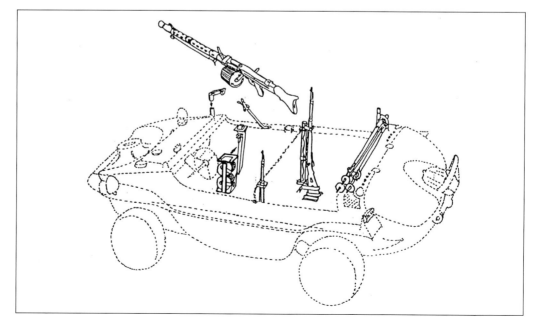

MG34 AND MG42 MACHINE GUNS

The MG34 and the MG42 were two of the finest machine guns of the Second World War, and indeed of the 20th century. They truly established the principle of the general-purpose machine gun (GPMG), an air-cooled firearm with a quick-change barrel and the ability to shift its purpose depending on the mount. While set on a standard bipod, for example, both guns could act as light machine guns for the infantry assault role, but fixed on tripod mounts they acted as medium machine guns to deliver sustained indirect fire. Introduced in 1934, the MG34 was a belt-fed short-recoil operated weapon that fired 7.92 × 57mm Mauser rounds at a cyclical rate of 800–900rpm. It was an extremely well-engineered weapon, with some sophisticated features. For example, it had a double-unit trigger in which squeezing the top half of the trigger gave single shots while drawing on the bottom half delivered full-auto fire. If anything, however, the MG34 was too refined for wartime production and use – it was expensive and time-consuming to manufacture and could be temperamental under dirty battlefield conditions. Thus in 1942 its official replacement appeared – the MG42. (Note that although the MG42 was meant to replace the MG34 in 1943, the latter weapon still served until the end of the war, particularly in vehicular and anti-aircraft

contexts.) The MG42 was also a belt-fed short-recoil operated firearm, but it was cheaper to manufacture, more durable, the barrel-change was even quicker (about 5 seconds in trained hands) and it delivered fire at a scorching 1,200rpm. The MG42 became much feared by the Allies, and such were the qualities of the weapon that it essentially still serves today, in modern versions such as the 7.62 × 51mm NATO MG3.

BELOW **This restored vehicle illustrates how heavily armed a Schwimmwagen could be. The weapons here are an MP40 sub-machine gun, two Panzerfausten and an MG34 machine gun.** *(Sean O'Flaherty)*

the weapon, standing behind the engine compartment of a stationary vehicle to give him maximum traverse.

In terms of ammunition stowage, the space between the rear deck lid of the Kübelwagen could be used to stow multiple 250-round *Patronenkasten* (ammunition boxes), and there were also clip mountings on the underside of the lid for holding both the single-barrel *Laufschützer 34* barrel container and its two-barrel equivalent, the *Laufbehälter 34*. When machine guns were actually mounted and used from the Kübelwagen, particularly from the swing-arm mount and the short rear pedestal, open belt feed was largely impractical. Given the motion of the vehicle and the configuration of the people within it, it was next to impossible to have a gunner's

assistant managing the flow of the belt into the gun. The ammunition was also likely to snag on parts of the vehicle, such as the lip of the folded-down windscreen.

For this reason, the Kübelwagen's machine guns were normally fed using the 50-round *Gurttrommel* (drum magazine), which could be used on the MG34 and 42. To carry several of the latter drums in a ready state, the Kübelwagen could fit a *Gurttrommelträgerlager* (drum magazine frame) on the inside of each rear door, using special mounting brackets. Similarly, the Schwimmwagen was fitted with frames next to the driver and his front passenger to carry four drum magazines (200 rounds) and the rear seats could be replaced with a rack holding 6 x 250-round ammunition cans.

ABOVE **This photograph from the North African theatre clearly shows the terrible terrain that Kübelwagen drivers had to negotiate.** *(BArch)*

BELOW **A group of Waffen-SS officers conduct a briefing around a Kübelwagen. Unusually, this vehicle has retained its hubcaps.**
(www.ww2incolour.com/Public Domain)

Combat crews

The Kübelwagen and Schwimmwagen were true front-line vehicles. Given their primary reconnaissance duties and the increasingly combative nature of German reconnaissance tactics as the war ground on, the vehicles often took on an offensive role, participating in direct attacks using either the hand-held weaponry stowed aboard or the mounted machine guns. During the operations in the Ardennes in 1944–45, we find examples of just how aggressive the crews of these light vehicles could be:

We drove in a Schwimmwagen through the forest and field trails to the battalion command post. We had to stop next to a couple of houses; the command post was also there. Four American tanks attacked and we had to seek cover in a nearby basement. The basement was already filled with Landser *[infantrymen]. The waiting and rattling of the tracks and the shouting made me nervous. I returned to the Schwimmwagen, where there were three Panzerfausten. I put them under my arm. Then I saw the four tanks standing and firing. I ran, ducking down, through a trench and approached to within 60–70m of the tanks. I cocked a Panzerfaust, aimed it at the largest, a Sherman, and pulled the trigger and it hit. The tank immediately blazed up. I marked the next tank, but, at the same moment, took fire and did not hit. I changed position, aimed and hit the next tank. Then the other two turned and left.*
(Quoted in Cooke and Evans, 2005, p. 148)

This quotation comes from one Helmut Merscher, a member of *Schnellgruppe Knittel* (Fast Group Knittel), a battlegroup built around *1. SS-Aufklärung* of the LSSAH. It shows how the Schwimmwagen could be used to take soldiers rapidly to forward positions, where they could engage the enemy at close quarters but then make a sharp exit once the damage had been done.

While there is no doubt an opportunistic aspect to the attack described above, the German collapse in the last months of the war led to both the Kübelwagen and Schwimmwagen taking a full assault role within mixed mechanised units, relying on their speed and manoeuvrability to steal a march on the enemy. In one account of the fighting on the Eastern Front in late 1944, Oberscharführer August Zinßmeister, a scouting party leader of the 12 SS-Panzer Division *Hitlerjugend*, described receiving orders for an attack:

> *15 December, Friday. In the evening we receive an order and are briefed in a neighbouring village held by units of Skorzeny, by one 'Dr. Wolf'. The overall order reads: The reinforced Panzer scouting party with three 'Pumas' and two rifle squads in Schwimmwagen will drive ahead of the spearheads of the advance unit. It will capture Ourthe bridge in a surprise raid, or reinforce paratroop units present there. It will hold that bridge as well as one Maas bridge south of Liège, in each case until our own spearhead arrives. We are enthusiastic, although we have some inkling of the difficulty of the mission. Eagerly and with great care we prepare for all possibilities and await the order to move out.*
> (Quoted in Hubert Meyer, 2005, pp. 235–36)

Here the Schwimmwagens are being used directly as the delivery mechanism for a bridge assault, backed by the heavier firepower of the *SdKfz* 234 Puma 8 × 8 armoured cars with their thumping cannon. Schwimmwagens were, as amphibious vehicles, well suited to bridge assaults, but indeed to any operation requiring the fast movement of small infantry units across water. With a forward-firing machine gun fitted, the vehicles could even provide their own suppressive fire while making the hazardous crossing.

Another fascinating example of the Kübelwagen and Schwimmwagen in combat comes again from the ranks of the Waffen-SS, this time from Kurt Meyer, the famous 'Panzer Meyer' commander. During the fighting around Kharkov in 1943, as leader of the SS-Panzergrenadier-Regiment 25, Meyer

ABOVE A Kübelwagen is used to transport Knight's Cross holder Oberleutnant Josef Gauglitz back into the battle in the Hürtgen Forest, December 1944. *(BArch)*

BELOW German police and army forces use a ferry to cross a river in Yugoslavia. The vehicle in the bottom left-hand corner is a Kübelwagen; note the absence of direction indicators, showing that this is a later model. *(BArch)*

RIGHT Motorcycle troops were terribly vulnerable to exposure on the Eastern Front during the winter, hence the Kübelwagen and Schwimmwagen were better suited to their reconnaissance duties. *(Cody Images)*

BELOW A Tiger tank of the SS-Panzer-Korps *Leibstandarte Adolf Hitler* rumbles past a Schwimmwagen in Normandy, 1944. *(BArch)*

described one notable action that occurred when an approaching Russian column was spotted:

> *At that point we consisted of four Schwimmwagen, a Kübelwagen and an eight-wheeled armoured car; in all we had twenty-three soldiers with four machine guns and individual pistols and rifles. This group of German soldiers observed a Russian march column from a distance of approximately 800 meters that consisted of thousands of Soviets and which had all types of weaponry with it. The terrain sloped gently down to the road and then climbed gently up the other side. While this side of the slope was covered with stands of trees, the far side opened up to an expanse of snow to the east which offered no cover. We did not stir in our positions. Observation posts would warn of approaching vehicles.*
>
> (Kurt Meyer, 2005, n.p.)

It was clear that this modest German force was outnumbered and materially outclassed by the Soviet column. Yet as so often occurred on the Eastern Front, German tactical bravado accomplished victories against disproportionate odds. A sudden air attack on the Soviet column by Ju 87 Stukas blew apart the column's integrity and it lost coherent communications. This was the moment to attack:

BELOW The tail light fitted on the upper right corner of the engine compartment was a feature of early Kübelwagens; it was omitted from vehicles produced from late 1942. *(Author's collection)*

I stared at that jumbled mass of humanity as it electrified. I grabbed a signal pistol from my vehicle and fired a red flare into the air. Bremer understood immediately. Stoll's section leapt into its vehicle and raced down the slope. The signals armoured car hammered its machine-gun fire into the Soviets and provided covering fire for us. We tore down the path shouting and yelling – in contravention of all conventional rules of warfare – our horns and sirens making a hellish din. We were attacking the Soviets! Red flares were still climbing high into the air. The Stukas had recognized us; they rocked their wings and stormed into the fleeing mass, sweeping the road clear with their guns.

(Kurt Meyer, 2005, n.p.)

The reference to both 'horns and sirens' is intriguing, leading one to speculate whether some of the vehicles were the Type 82/2, which were fitted with Siemens motor-driven sirens mounted on the passenger side, in place of the rear seat. Whatever the case, the combined confusion of a sudden air attack, plus the rapid, swarming manoeuvres of the Schwimmwagen and the Kübelwagen, rout a far larger enemy, illustrating that the value of these vehicles lay not just in the way that they were built, but also the innovation and bravado with which they were used.

It is all too easy to get carried away with such

stirring narratives. Yet as a counterbalance, we have to recognise that the Kübelwagen and Schwimmwagen were extremely vulnerable vehicles. During the research for this book, I came across numerous cursory accounts from Allied soldiers referring to destroying such vehicles easily with bursts of small-arms fire. Across all fronts, particularly between 1944 and 1945, the Kübelwagen and Schwimmwagen crews also became dreadfully exposed to air attack from predatory fighter-bombers, as the collapsing Luftwaffe lost its air superiority.

ABOVE Soldiers march alongside a Kübelwagen on a hot day in Yugoslavia. The Kübelwagen's crawler gear meant it could keep perfect pace with marching troops. *(BArch)*

BELOW Allied air power became a terrible danger for German vehicle crews in France in 1944. Here a Kübelwagen passenger observes the sky nervously while others watch a strafed-up column burn. *(BArch)*

Rare photographs of such vehicles after being strafed remind us that both the Kübelwagen and Schwimmwagen offered almost no resistance to bullets or shell fragments; an on-target half-second burst from a P-47 Thunderbolt or a Hawker Typhoon could literally rip the vehicle apart like a cheap tin can. Both the Kübelwagen and Schwimmwagen were designed for manoeuvrability, not protection.

The fate of many wartime vehicles, however, was not to be destroyed but to fall into the hands of the enemy. One poignant account of such a transition comes from Reinhold Busch, a survivor of Stalingrad, who here recounts what happened with the final German capitulation in the battle in early 1943:

After a while my friend from the mot.–unit returned with the news that Paulus had capitulated and we all had to go into captivity. As a soldier mindful of his duty my friend wanted to immobilize his vehicle. While debating with himself whether to use a round set hammer or hand grenade, I looked at my poor feet and suggested that the four of us should drive into captivity rather than walk. No sooner said than done: we got in. Thus we four friends drove at marching pace in our Kübelwagen, amidst the countless shambling companions sharing our fate, towards an uncertain future in captivity.

When we met our first Russian, an officer, he slipped his long legs nimbly into the Kübelwagen without making us stop. Hooting the horn on the orders of this officer, we made much better progress, and we overtook the columns of prisoners streaming north-east away from the city. After a few kilometres a little outside the city where the road forked our comfortable journey came to an end.

The Russian made us stop and gestured to us 54ers [54th Regiment] that we should get out. Then he told our host from the motorized unit to drive on as his chauffeur! At the same moment as he roared off hooting the horn again, we were surrounded by Russians who robbed us of watches and lighters with loud 'Urr jest!' and 'Mashinka jest!'

(Busch, 2014, p. 214)

There is something undoubtedly moving about the 'four friends' in the space of their Kübelwagen, travelling in the crawler gear towards captivity and a frankly appalling future. The Russian officer who took the Kübelwagen doubtless inherited a vehicle that served him well for weeks or months to come, until mechanical neglect probably led to its final breakdown and abandonment.

Allied analysis

The Allies naturally took great interest in the design of all German military vehicles, and the Kübelwagen and Schwimmwagen were no exception. In fact, both vehicles, but particularly the Kübelwagen, seemed to offer something of a challenge to Allied thinking. Much about the Kübelwagen's design – its lightness, the rear-mounted and air-cooled engine, its excellent cross-country mobility – challenged the design principles of many Allied vehicles within the same vehicular categories, vehicles that were often heavier, more expensive and less reliable.

Allied assessors of the Kübelwagen are often torn between expressing praise for individual features against an overall resistance to classifying it as superior, or at least equivalent to,

ABOVE Luftwaffe troops in Kübelwagens in North Africa. Note the protective cover over the spare wheel, to protect the rubber from sun damage. *(BArch)*

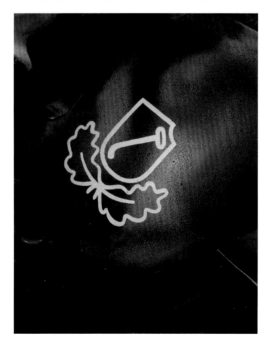

LEFT Vehicle insignia of the 1 SS-Panzer Division, as displayed on the front mudguard of a restored Kübelwagen. *(Author's collection)*

standard British or American vehicles. A good example of this patriotic conflict comes from a wartime *Autocar* report by journalist and British Army captain John Dugdale, dated 17 October 1941. After delivering what was a fairly positive review of a captured Kübelwagen, he works up to pronouncing his final judgement:

Finally, important design that the Volkswagen is when it is remembered that it is the considered result of eminent technicians' research over a long and unrestricted period, it is evident that it is a civilian car and not an Army vehicle. It was noticed that the parking brake handle had been practically torn in half by some hearty driver.

The British Army vehicle [it isn't entirely clear to which specific vehicle Dugdale is alluding], which may not have such modern refinements as four-wheel independent suspension and a rear engine, is certainly at least strong enough to withstand the sturdy handling of our desert boys. The result of a British Army driver being put in charge of a German Army Volkswagen is unpleasant to contemplate. This altogether too delicate piece of equipment is one more pointer towards the inevitable fact that Germany is having to make do with what material she can get hold of. Not even the stencilled 'Afrika Korps' sign turns the People's Car into a desert buggy, as we call our trucks.

(Dugdale, *Autocar*, 17 October 1941)

Many faultlines run through this final assessment, even giving some allowance for the constraints of wartime propaganda. One is that Dugdale does not seem to consider that the vehicle's very lightness, or 'delicacy' as he might put it, is part of a conscious effort to limit body weight and therefore improve traction and performance characteristics. He also doesn't reflect on the fact that by this stage of the war the Kübelwagen had already proved that it was capable of handling rough combat conditions, both in North Africa and the Eastern Front. Dugdale seems largely to take the example of an admittedly flimsy handbrake as representative of a more general tendency to mechanical failure.

Similar examples of basic wartime prejudice are found in other British and American reviews of the Kübelwagen, yet there is no doubt that both nations respected the vehicle and found much to admire. For a start, both Britain and the United States produced very extensive technical reports based on captured Kübelwagens. The major British report was that published by the British Intelligence Objectives Sub-committee (BIOS) via engineers at the Humber vehicle manufacturing company. There was also a short manual on the Type 82 from the British Army (Handbook 87). The Americans went even further, producing an entire technical manual – TM E9-803 – in 1944. All of these works provide invaluable insight into the

LEFT This North African Kübelwagen has an early type of rear body, with just a small central protection pan underneath featuring an aperture for crank starter access. *(BArch)*

construction of wartime Kübelwagens, and have been quoted extensively here. Yet the American manual was more than just an evaluation of an enemy vehicle; it was also an instruction book for actual use. Both the British and the Americans used captured Kübelwagens to supplement their own vehicles, the British first acquiring them in North Africa and the Americans in the later stages of the North Africa campaign and subsequently in Italy and western Europe. Rebranded with prominent British and

LEFT The Kübelwagen floor was fitted with duckboards to keep the occupants' boots out of dirt and water. *(Author's collection)*

LEFT A Waffen-SS reconnaissance force deploys a Pak 38 anti-tank gun forward, while a Kübelwagen driver observes from behind. *(BArch)*

Volkswagen', a Willys Jeep and a Kübelwagen are pictured together in a photograph, with the following text:

Here, side by side, you see the two most popular vehicles of the war – one, an American jeep; the other, the German Volkswagen. They answer many questions about the relative quality of German and American vehicles. Captured Volkswagens have been tested and they are nothing to brag about. They have a two-wheel drive and the jeep drive is four-wheel. Their top speed is thirty miles per hour and the jeep's is fifty. Their suspension and general construction doesn't permit the tough cross-country driving the jeep can take. What's true of these cars is pretty true of German and American trucks, personnel carriers and tractors. We make them better as well as faster.

German cars and motorcycles travel about thirty-eight miles an hour alone; in convoy speed drops to about twenty-two miles an hour under good conditions. Trucks travel twenty-five miles an hour alone and twenty-two in convoy. Tanks generally travel fifteen miles an hour alone and eleven in convoy.

For years Hitler has been promising the Germans a car in every garage, and has deducted vast funds from people's pay as advance payments on these cars. The German people never did get their cars — for the entire production was intended for the army from the very beginning. The German soldier, however, figures that the car is his, bought and paid for, so he takes very good care of it as well as any other vehicles entrusted to his care. German lubricants and gasolines are quite good. But the main reason for the success of German motorized equipment in campaigns ranging from the plains of Poland to the mountains of Greece is preventive maintenance by the German soldier.

(Director of Military Training, Army Service Forces, 1944)

American insignia, these vehicles appear to have given dependable service. As we have already seen, the Soviets also utilised captured Kübelwagens, appreciating their excellent off-road capabilities.

One particular focus of wartime – and indeed post-war – assessment of the Kübelwagen is to make a comparison with the US ¼-ton Command and Reconnaissance Truck, 4 × 4 – otherwise known as the Jeep. Manufactured by Willys-Overland (as the Model MB) and Ford (Model GPW), the Jeep was mechanically a different beast to the Kübelwagen. It was a 4 × 4 vehicle with a front-mounted 54hp four-cylinder water-cooled engine, with three forward gears and one reverse gear. Suspension was provided by longitudinal semi-elliptical leaf springs. The build quality of the Jeep was more substantial than the Kübelwagen – the vehicle weighed 1,113kg (2,453lb) empty, as opposed to the mere 725kg (1,598lb) of the Kübelwagen.

A flavour of the competition between the Jeep and the Kübelwagen comes from an American article in *The German Soldier*, a booklet published by the *Infantry Journal* in 1943. In the appropriately entitled 'Jeep vs.

As before, we have to make allowances for the needs of propaganda – praising the quality of the enemy's vehicles wouldn't be good for

morale, especially amongst new recruits (the intended readership of the booklet). There are some evident untruths – the Kübelwagen could do 80km/h (50mph) as its top speed, and it could also handle some very rough terrain. Preventive maintenance was indeed important to the successful running of the Kübelwagen, but show me the military vehicle where it isn't.

Where the two vehicles were similar was that both actually had the same sort of rugged reliability and off-road confidence. If anything, the Jeep was 'tougher' than the Kübelwagen in blunt physical terms, and could carry a heavier payload, but the Kübelwagen was just as nimble without the greater demand on industrial resources.

Comparing the Jeep to the Schwimmwagen is also illuminating, as the latter offered the four-wheel-drive capability of the Jeep, plus added an amphibious capability. One of the most judicious comparative analyses of the Schwimmwagen is found in a US SAE War Engineering Board report dated August 1945. Hostilities with Germany might have ended, but US military engineers were eagerly exploring the technicalities of German war materiel, and the Schwimmwagen came in for attention. The

ABOVE US airborne soldiers commandeer a Luftwaffe Kübelwagen in the streets of Carentan, Normandy, 1944. With the spare wheel removed, the wheel mount is visible. *(NARA)*

BELOW British airborne troops cross back over the Rhine in a captured German Kübelwagen, 24–25 March 1945. Kübelwagens were especially popular vehicles for scavenging Allied soldiers in search of transport. *(Crown Copyright)*

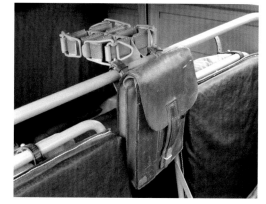

general conclusion about the overall quality of the vehicle is a balanced one:

American vehicles because of their surplus power can always do more than they were designed for. However, in the judgement of the committee this vehicle has sufficient power for its intended purpose, namely, that of a reconnaissance vehicle in which it may be called on to cross ponds, small lakes and rivers, soft ground etc. More power would mean the necessity of larger component parts, which would mean that the vehicle could lose many of its outstanding characteristics. If this vehicle had the power plant of an American Jeep it would probably mean that its weight would go up to that of the standard Jeep.

The vehicle has a decided weight advantage which is valuable for an amphibious vehicle. There are important lessons in the reduction and saving of weight in this vehicle, especially in the engine and the hull construction.

The American Amphibious Jeep weighs approximately 3400 pounds compared to slightly more than 1700 pounds for the German amphibious Volkswagen. Pounds per horsepower without load are about the same for this vehicle and the American Jeep.

In the judgement of members of this committee who have driven all U.S. amphibious vehicles, the general handling, steering and controlling of this vehicle with the use of the front wheels as a rudder, are superior to that of the U.S. amphibious vehicles.

(SAE War Engineering Board, 1945, p. 6)

LEFT A restored Kübelwagen. The front bumper bar was fitted on vehicles from late 1943 to early 1944. *(Author's collection)*

The US engineers, after consideration, accept that the light weight of the Schwimmwagen compared to many US vehicles does not equate with flimsiness, but rather with performance. Their central point is that the power output and body weight of the Schwimmwagen are actually perfectly suited to the specific roles demanded of the vehicle, with the implication that structural strengthening and power output increase would be unnecessary. Note especially how the committee recognise that both the Schwimmwagen and the Jeep share the same power-per-vehicle-pound, hence the two vehicles were able to deliver similar off-road performance despite the signal differences in engine and configuration. The last judgement in this passage is telling, and it would be interesting to know how well this report's conclusions were received along the corridors of power in the US defence administration.

Yet the overarching point about the Jeep/ Kübelwagen/Schwimmwagen comparisons is industrial rather than technological. The United States had the resources and budget to produce Jeeps in vast numbers – 634,569 vehicles (both Wilys MBs and Ford GPWs), a figure that totally eclipses the output of Kübelwagens and Schwimmwagens. It was

WARTIME PRODUCTION CONDITIONS

The production of wartime Kübelwagen and Schwimmwagen vehicles came at a high price to the actual wartime VW workforce. From 1940 until 1945, the proportion of forced labour at the VW plant at Fallersleben grew inexorably, rising from 919 foreign workers in 1940 to 11,041 by 1943. Many of the workers were engineering or mechanical professionals from Russia and Poland, either captured soldiers or civilians displaced into camps by German occupation, but an especially high proportion was Italian. Special 'recruiters' from VW and military authorities would select the individuals on the basis of their professional past, and put them to work at Fallersleben under extremely harsh conditions. Beatings were common and productivity targets were almost always impossibly high. Food was frequently in short supply. Some 650 women, mostly Hungarian Jews taken from Auschwitz-Birkenau but also others from Bergen-Belsen, were from August 1944 used in armaments production at the plant, housed in a converted shower hall. As a result of sexual abuse by the guards, many had children, most of whom died of neglect in the factory's 'children's home'. In 1999, a memorial was established on the premises of the VW factory, remembering some 20,000 forced labourers who toiled in the factory during the war years.

therefore not uncommon for German soldiers to be seen riding around in captured Jeeps. In no sense should this be read as an adverse verdict upon the Kübelwagen. The Kübelwagen and Schwimmwagen were produced in very small numbers considering the scale of the German requirement, and by acquiring a Jeep the Wehrmacht troops had a vehicle that had cross-country superiority compared to many other vehicles in the German inventory.

Post-war runners

One point that leans against Allied low opinions of the Kübelwagen was that it actually continued in production for a short time following the end of the war. In total, 1,785 Kübelwagens were built in Germany specifically for the British occupation forces between May and December 1945.

Yet notwithstanding new production vehicles, liberated Europe was awash with military surplus vehicles of all shades and hues, and

the Kübelwagen and Schwimmwagen were amongst those used by both civilian and soldier alike. A particularly interesting assessment of a Kübelwagen and a Schwimmwagen came courtesy of *Autocar* once again, this time from journalist H.E. Ellis, who managed to indulge his passion for all things vehicular on the roads of newly liberated Normandy:

While wandering among the bewildering assortment of vehicles I came across a captured Volkswagen *and a German version of the amphibious Jeep, both in running order. I persuaded the officer-in-charge to allow me to drive both these cars and was somewhat surprised about the 'people's car'. First, it is extremely flimsy – in fact, tinny – and the low weight thus obtained gives it very good acceleration; secondly, it handles remarkably well. The engine is quite flexible and the suspension and seating seemed, from my short experience of the car, to make for comfortable riding. The rear engine practically eliminates noise and heat in the driving compartment and the gear box is reasonably good. I 'nursed' it up to about 40 m.p.h., but I have no doubt that in proper shape it would exceed this speed.*

If one took this badly knocked about example of the Volkswagen *as a criterion I would say that, if one is prepared to put up with a car that rattles like fury and has absolutely no refinements, then the* Volkswagen *is not at all a bad car. But it is definitely not my idea of what I want for my wife and family* après la guerre.

The German amphibious car is a quite heavy, robustly constructed affair for its size and did not appear to be very fast. For land use the water propeller and rudder unit is hinged to swing upwards and away from the drive shaft, which projects through a gland at the rear of the hull or body. On the amphibious Jeep the propeller and rudder are fixed.

(Ellis, *Autocar*, 1944)

The tone of this article alone is interesting. With victory almost assured, you sense that the writer now permits himself to be freer with praise of German vehicles, unlike those reviewers writing in the more anxious days of 1941–43. Consequently,

Ellis is quite effusive about the Kübelwagen, noting its acceleration, comfort, engineering and general performance as being of a good standard, although only for a military vehicle and not for a civilian ride. About the Schwimmwagen he is rather neutral, and comes across as less technically conversant with the vehicle. He states, for example, that the Schwimmwagen has a 'rudder unit', confusing the propeller housing with a directional fitting. He compares the Schwimmwagen, without judgement, to the Ford GPA 'Seep' (Sea Jeep), a rather unsuccessful amphibious version of the Ford GPW Jeep.

In Chapter 1, we looked closely at two particular post-war derivations of the Kübelwagen – the Type 181 and the Australian Country Buggy. So what were these vehicles like to drive? Did they successfully marry post-war civilian comfort with the Kübelwagen's off-road performance and resilience?

In October 1973, the British *Custom Car* magazine did a road test of the Type 181, bringing it together with an original Type 82 for comparison. On the whole, the reviewer ('R.P.') was more than impressed with the new car. He noted that the bodywork remained pressed steel, although of stronger build than the Type 82 – 'the metal is double-skinned round the rear portion of the body and down the sills on either side of the lower body. This gives it real rigidity with the four door-apertures and no top to keep it together.' Another interesting passage from the review elaborates on some of the features that add to the vehicle's comfort:

The comfortable seats are from the VW saloon, and so are most of the instruments including the light controls, speedo and tank gauge. A couple of novelties on the dash you won't find on the ordinary Beetle range, however, are the electrical socket for plugging in a shaver, inspection lamp or perhaps a kettle, and the gas heater found in the 411 range. Useful things, gas heaters. They run off the vehicle's fuel by drawing petrol into the heater, vaporising it, and burning it with a jumbo sparking plug. This huffs out the proverbial dragon's breath when it's switched on and roars out of a tunnel under the dash panel. The heater is controlled by a timer in the switch, and can be used to heat up the interior before the car is driven, a touch of luxury if ever there was one. Throughout the handbook references are made to operating in arctic conditions and this heater is just what you need to keep your toes aglow if you fancy a drive up to the 16th parallel.

(*Custom Car*, 1973)

LEFT A French nurse is hard at work adapting a captured Kübelwagen as a medical vehicle in France, 1944.
(www.stolly.org.uk)

ABOVE **The VW Type 181, otherwise known as 'The Thing'. Although derived from the Kübelwagen, it had many differences, not least that the Kübelwagen's exposed spare wheel was now hidden away.** *(Sven Storbeck)*

The reference to arctic driving is a reminder that the Type 181, like its wartime ancestor, was intended for rough riding and hard knocks in adverse conditions. The reviewer notes that the collapsible hood and sidescreen windows fit nice and snugly to keep out unwelcome draughts. He also explains that 'Our 181 was wearing Continental 16.5 x 15 mud and snow tyres which should see it through most conditions, especially as it's so light [the vehicle had a kerb weight of 910kg/2,006lb] at well under a ton. Most FWD vehicles are rather heavy and they really need their front-driven axle to compensate' (*Custom Car*, 1973). The fact that the Type 181 was heavier than the Type 82 by nearly 200kg (440lb) was not a problem

given the Type 181's powerplant: 'If the original engine was good, then today's 1600 twin-port mill must be fine for the 181. It has twice the power of its elderly relative, giving The Thing the performance of a Beetle with a high cruising speed and plenty of performance for off-road work.' If anything, the reviewer would like more of a return to the styling of the original car, observing that the fuel tank and the spare wheel are now located up front under the bonnet, 'much to the dismay of Kübel enthusiasts, who would like to see it out on the bonnet like the original' (*Custom Car*, 1973).

So, in general a big thumbs up for the Type 181, and many other users concurred. Yet not all was well. In 1973, American automobile activist Ralph Nader headed a campaign against the Type 181 to have it banned from importation into the United States. The vehicle (or rather Volkswagen of America) was even given the crowning position at the Second Annual Automotive Engineering Malpractice Award, run by the Washington DC-based Center for Automotive Safety. The Center's director, Lowell Dodge, publicly branded the vehicle as unsafe, or at least well below federal safety standards.

A storm was brewing, and Volkswagen did not take it lying down. On 6 August 1973, Arthur R. Railton of Volkswagen America, no stranger to taking on an occasionally adverse press, delivered a sharp written response to Nader and Dodge, which included the following factual riposte:

BELOW **The military Type 181 sits alongside other West German army vehicles. One clear difference from the Kübelwagen are the unidirectional opening doors.** *(Frank Schwichtenberg/Creative Commons Licence)*

Mr. Dodge seems to be charging that Volkswagen is guilty of producing an unsafe vehicle or of trying somehow to get around the safety standards. Here are some facts he failed to mention:

1. *The Department of Transportation approved the designation as multi-purpose.*
2. *The Department of Transportation has approved other well-known vehicles under the same designation: the Jeep, Bronco, Scout, Toyota Land Cruiser, Blazer. All these vehicles meet the same safety-standard requirements as The Thing, no more, no less.*
3. *The Thing was developed in the early 1960s as an off-road vehicle for NATO forces in Europe and is not something VW concocted to circumvent safety standards. Unlike all the above (except the Jeep) it started out to be an off-road vehicle.*
4. *The Thing meets all safety standards that apply to such vehicles.*
5. *The Thing is not a 'cosmetic' off-road vehicle. Here are some features that make it an exceptional off-road machine:*
   a. *Ground clearance: 8.1 inches*
   b. *Angle of approach: 36 degrees*
   c. *Angle of departure: 31 degrees*
   d. *Fording (pardon the expression, Henry) depth: 15.6 inches*
   e. *Engine protection shield*
   f. *Towing eyes, front and rear*

g. *Lower overall transmission/final drive – hill-climbing capability 15% greater than the Beetle*
h. *Reinforced suspension front and rear*
i. *Off-road type air cleaner*
j. *Five-inch wide rims with Radial mud and snow tires standard*

It is most interesting that the award Mr. Dodge presented to us has Jeep as its centrepiece. There are many times more Jeeps on the road than 'Things' – yet I noticed no presentation of malpractice awards to American Motors.

(VW America, Railton, 1973)

America of the 1970s was a generally combative time and place for Volkswagen. In 1971 a study conducted by several US agencies produced a report that seemed to suggest that small, foreign

ABOVE A Kübelwagen driver changes a flat tyre, using the jack stowed on the left side of the engine compartment, fitted into the aperture in the body frame. (BArch)

LEFT A rather forlorn-looking VW Type 181. In their prime, however, 'The Thing' gave a respectable performance from its 1,600cc engine. (Source: Tavogalarza via Wikimedia Commons)

ABOVE In this rear view of a restored Kübelwagen, we see the bumper rod fitted to late-model vehicles. Note that the drop-down reflector seen at the very bottom of the picture was present on all models. *(Author's collection)*

rush of foreign imports was starting to eat into the balance sheets of the big American motor manufacturers. The report placed Volkswagen in the spotlight, putting their vehicles in 20.6% of the total number of accidents resulting in death or serious injury, the highest of all manufacturers. Railton waded into this discussion publicly, and dismissed claims that rear-engine instability was to blame for many of the crashes. Nevertheless, time ran out for The Thing in 1975, when it was no longer imported into the United States because of its failure to meet new safety restrictions. One point to note, of relevance to the safety debate, was that an analysis of Type 181 owners' reports from 1972 to 1973 indicated that 50.3% of the drivers were aged 15–29 years and 43% aged 30–49 years. The Thing was certainly a young person's car.

It is also worth mentioning something about the service of the Australian Country Buggy. As Chapter 1 pointed out, the Country Buggy was very much a no-frills vehicle, retailing at the time for about £725. Performance was sedentary to say the least – to climb from 25 to 35mph took a blistering 10 seconds, and 0–60 was almost measured in minutes. One reviewer of the vehicle, D. Penhale, writing for *VW Safer Motoring*, noted that 'The basic unit is the VW sedan chassis, gearbox, engine, front and rear suspension and wheels. Upon this has been erected a well made sheet metal body something like, but not very much, the Afrika Korps (Kubelwagen) vehicle in World War II.' The reviewer took his test vehicle on both the road and in cross-country conditions. On the road the vehicle 'proved to be comfortable and pleasant to drive', but off-road Penhale had some reservations:

imported cars were more likely to be involved in serious accidents resulting in fatalities or significant injury than big cars. The report was a political hot potato, coming at a time when the

BELOW The Country Buggy was a post-war Australian reimagining of the Kübelwagen, albeit one that had limited commercial success during the 1960s and '70s. *(Ferenghi)*

BELOW RIGHT A VW Country Buggy, with its forebear – the VW Beetle – in the background. Note the complete absence of doors, replaced by roll-down canopies. *(Ferenghi)*

Performance in farm conditions was measured near to a local hill climb. The Buggy, in second gear, trickled up and down the steep inclines always under control, its nine inch ground clearance enabling it to easily avoid an abundance of rocky outcrops. But a combination of a thin layer of sand over seaweed and wintertread tyres proved the Country Buggy's downfall when I went to the beach to see how it performed. As these conditions are rare I would predict perfect manners in inland sand areas using types suitable to those conditions.

(Penhale, 'Testing the factory-made Bush Buggy in Australian Sheep Country', in *VW Safer Motoring*, December 1968)

The reviewer is judicious in his comments, noting that even an off-road vehicle needs to be configured properly, particularly in terms of tyres, if it is to perform. There had been some problems, however, that couldn't be remedied with just a tyre change. Following an evaluation in January 1968, a collection of faults with the vehicle were identified. Some were minor – there were slight problems with water leakage at the joins between the body and the hood, and the plastic side curtains shrank, making it difficult to use the zipper fastenings. Other issues were more substantial – these included spring plates breaking and body panels cracking after hard off-road use. Yet all these problems were remedied before the vehicle officially went on sale in April 1968. Good reviews and decent performance, however, could not save the Country Buggy from commercial realities in Australia. Restored versions are still running, not only in Australia but also throughout the Philippines, where they are often fitted with different car bodies to repurpose them as two-door coupés.

As we have seen, the Kübelwagen and Schwimmwagen have had a lively history in both war and peace. Hundreds of the vehicles still survive today in the hands of restorers and enthusiasts, so the rattle of the air-cooled VW motor can still be heard. Given the durability of these vehicles – contrary to what Allied commentators said during the war – that noise is likely to continue for some time.

LEFT The Australian VW Country Buggy was rechristened the 'Sakbayan' in the Philippines. Today the vehicles mainly exist within the context of car clubs. *(Volkswagen)*

TRACKS VS WHEELS

A perennial debate amongst the developers of military vehicles relates to the argued advantages and disadvantages of wheels vs tracks. Tracks undoubtedly excel in off-road mobility over diverse terrain types, by virtue of the wider distribution of the vehicle's ground pressure plus the far larger contact area provided by a long track, thereby increasing traction. This is why main battle tanks (MBTs), the heaviest of all military vehicles, invariably opt for track systems. Tracked vehicles are also less vulnerable to battle damage than wheeled vehicles – the heavy metal-link tracks and steel wheels shrug off small-arms fire that would shred a wheeled vehicle's tyres or damage the suspension. (Modern systems such as run-flat tyres have gone a long way to improving the combat durability of wheeled vehicles, however.) Another interesting point in favour of tracked vehicles is that they are actually inherently more compact than wheeled vehicles, because of factors such as the absence of drive shafts and transfer cases. The compactness serves to lower the profile, hence making the vehicle more survivable. However, the case for tracked vehicles is not entirely clear-cut. Wheeled vehicles provide better on-road speed, which can be very important for rapid theatre deployments, and wheels are more durable for long road journeys than tracks. Wheels also inflict less damage on road and track surfaces. Wheeled vehicles tend to be less punishing on the driver and other occupants in terms of physical fatigue, because of the suspension system and the cushioning provided by pneumatic tyres, and they typically have far lower fuel and operating costs than tracked vehicles. The decision between wheels or tracks is therefore a finely balanced one. Some modern studies suggest that if a vehicle will spend more than 60% of its operational life off-road, tracks are the best option.

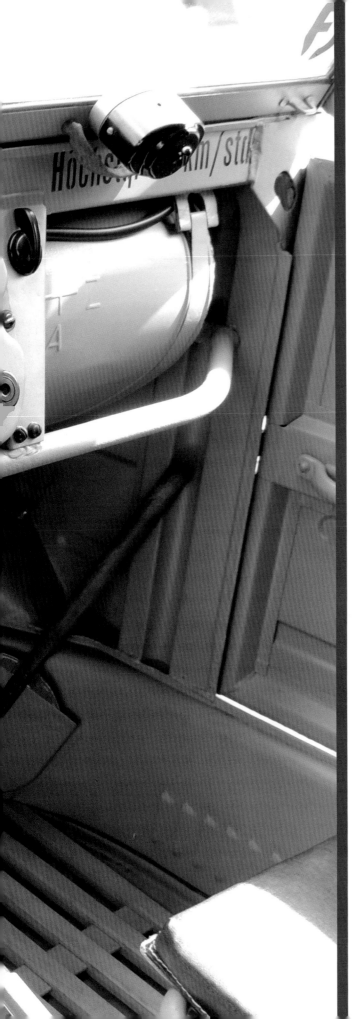

Chapter Five

The driver's view

───●───

The Kübelwagen and
Schwimmwagen did not promise
anything approaching comfort
and luxury. They were spartan
vehicles, and their wartime
drivers needed to be tough and
self-reliant.

OPPOSITE This photograph gives a good perspective on the
driver's view of the Kübelwagen. The steering wheel had a
Bakelite rim and spokes, but was replaced with a cheaper
metal-spoke version from mid-1942. *(Author's collection)*

The Wehrmacht took vehicles and drivers very seriously indeed. Although the German armed services never achieved their intended levels of mechanisation during the war, their tactical and logistical efficacy still depended upon the skills and endurance of hundreds of thousands of drivers, handling everything from motorbikes to Tiger tanks. Drivers were not just personnel manning a wheel and pointing a vehicle in the right direction. They had to be good soldiers who understood the tactical implications of every turn or parking stop. They had to keep their vehicles going under the most extreme environmental pressures, hence they were often as much engineers as they were drivers. They also had to be survivors, as vehicles naturally drew the attention of enemy guns and aircraft.

In this chapter, we will look more closely at the driver's experience of the Kübelwagen and Schwimmwagen. This examination falls roughly into two parts. First, we will explore what it actually meant to be a driver of these vehicles, and what life was like for such individuals. Second, we will assess the driving characteristics of the Kübelwagen and Schwimmwagen, particularly under extreme battlefield conditions. As we shall see, the rather humble vehicles contained individuals who often had to do extraordinary things.

The driver's role

The drivers of the Kübelwagen and Schwimmwagen would have held a *Wehrmacht-Führerschein* (Armed Forces Driver's Licence), a four-page certificate printed on grey oilcloth, which showed that he had received the appropriate training to

man a military vehicle. (During the pre-war years this document was known as the *Militärführerschein*, and some older drivers would still have carried these during the war.) One notable point is that many military licence holders would not necessarily have held a civilian driver's licence – given the relative scarcity of privately held motor vehicles in pre-war Germany, for many men their first experience of driving was in a military vehicle.

One useful source of trained drivers for the Wehrmacht was the Nationalsozialistisches Kraftfahrkorps (NSKK; National Socialist Motor Corps), established in 1931. The NSKK was originally part of the Sturmabteilung (SA), but managed to survive Hitler's swathing purge of that organisation in 1934 and went on to become an independent body dedicated to training drivers for armoured and motorised units. The NSKK did the Wehrmacht a valuable service at the beginning of the war by providing 200,000 men who had undertaken a five-month driving and mechanics course, and it burgeoned throughout the war not only as a source of driver training but also as a provider of operational units.

In active service a Kübelwagen and Schwimmwagen driver would have the chance, from 23 October 1942, to obtain a *Kraftfahrbewährungsabzeichen* (Motor Vehicle Driver's Proficiency Badge). These were available to all Wehrmacht personnel, including civilians and also foreign volunteers, who had demonstrated driving ability, personal courage and mechanical diligence in front-line combat for a prescribed number of days. (Note that the awards were retroactive back to 1 December 1940.) Three grades of award were available – gold, silver and bronze – and they came with an accompanying certificate.

There were typically plenty of opportunities for Kübelwagen and Schwimmwagen drivers to attain such awards, considering the length of the campaigns and of the conflict itself. As outlined in Chapter 4, the drivers of these light vehicles could find themselves performing roles ranging from transporting a field commander between headquarters to engaging in fast assault missions against defined enemy positions. Yet amidst all their operational duties, the drivers also had to keep their respective

LEFT A Luftwaffe man poses in front of his Kübelwagen in Tunisia. It must be remembered that many of the men who drove such vehicles were in their late teens and early twenties. *(BArch)*

BELOW A heavily camouflaged Kübelwagen in Normandy in 1944. Many pictures from the Western Front in 1944 show at least one vehicle occupant scanning the skies for enemy aircraft. *(BArch)*

GERMAN VEHICLE NUMBER PLATES

German vehicle number plates were given a suffix to designate the branch of service. These suffixes were:

WH – Wehrmacht Heer (Army)
WL – Wehrmacht Luftwaffe (Air Force)
WM – Wehrmacht Marine (Navy)
SS – Waffen-SS
POL – Polizei (Police)
OT – Organisation Todt

The last prefix was changed to WT in 1944, when the Todt organisation was absorbed into the Wehrmacht. Note also that Wehrmacht number plates normally carried (as a security measure) a red stamp identifying the *Feldpostnummer* (Field Post Office Number) of the unit to which the vehicle belonged.

paperwork in order. The German forces seemed to exhibit a superhuman capacity to maintain administration (and to generate paperwork) even under the most calamitous conditions, and Kübelwagen and Schwimmwagen drivers were no exception.

In terms of vehicle-related documents, the following were normally carried within the VW, in a canvas or leather pouch:

- ■ *Kraftfahrzeugschein* (Registration Certificate). A four-page card, it showed the licence plate and other key vehicle registration data plus the *Feldpostnummer* of the unit.
- ■ *Begleitheft* (Technical Log Book). This important little book described in detail all the tools and accessories carried on the vehicle. It was checked and signed for by the unit taking possession of the vehicle and at vehicle inspections. It also contained details of technical inspections, as well as regular services, overhauls and oil changes. Major changes to the vehicle were also recorded in the Vehicle Record Book (Kfz Buch) which was kept at the divisional depot.
- ■ *Fahrtnachweis* (Vehicle Journey Log). This was a booklet detailing every journey made by the vehicle – where to and where from, together with details of distance travelled and fuel consumed, all duly signed by the driver and countersigned by the driver's superior. The booklet recorded the details of 25 journeys, at which point the book was fully completed, and the total distance travelled and the fuel use would be calculated to indicate kilometres travelled per litre of fuel. The details would be recorded in the unit's Fuel Record Register and would show up any irregularities in fuel consumption.
- ■ *Fahrbefehl* (Trip Ticket). This was a single-sheet form, bearing an authorised signature and detailing the date, the vehicle, the driver, where from, where to, the purpose of the journey and approximate distance. It also

— 3 —

1. Beschreibung

Bezeichnung des Kraftfahrzeuges:	Abgekürzte Bezeichnung:	Anf. Nr.	Verladeklasse für Eisenbahntransport
laufer gel. *Personenkraftwagen*	*l. gl. Pkw*	*HHO*	*III*

Herstellungsjahr	*1935*			
Auf dem Rahmen und Haspel eingeschlagene Kontroll-Nr.	*64072*	Achsstand m	0 ——— 0	
Art des Aufbaues	*Kübel*		0 — 0 — 0 v. m. h.	
Eigengewicht, betriebsfertig . kg	*730*	Radbreite {größtes Außenmaß	vorn mm hinten mm	
Höchstgewicht, beladen . . . . kg	*1280*	Spurweite von Mitte zu Mitte Reifen {einfach	vorn m *1,15* hinten m *1,22*	
Achsdruck {beladen {vorn kg / hinten kg / unbeladen {vorn kg / hinten kg		{doppelt	inn. Reifen m	
			hinten {äuß. Reifen m	
		Bodenfreiheit mm	*200*	
Beförderungsmöglichkeit (Personen ohne Bedienungspersonal)		Bauchfreiheit mm		
Straße	*2*	Oeffnung des Zughakens . mm		
Gelände . . .	*2*	Höhe der Anhängevorrichtung über der Fahrbahn . . . . mm		
Tragfähigkeit in kg {Straße . . . . . / Gelände . .		Zugkraft am Zughaken kg . .		
		Durchschnittsgeschwindigkeit km-Std. {Straße	*60*	
		{Gelände	*30*	
Laderaum {Länge m . . / Breite m . . / Höhe m . .		Mittlere Tagesleistung in km {Straße . . .	*300*	
		{Gelände	*150*	
		{Feldwege . . .	*200*	
Größte Außenmaße {Länge m . *3,60* / Breite m . *1,50* / Höhe m . *1,66*		Fassungsvermögen des {Kraftstoffbehälters l	*35*	
		{Ölbehälters a. Motor l	*4*	

LEFT One of the early pages of the *Begleitheft für Kraftfahrzeuge*, a document that contained technical information about the vehicle. *(Courtesy Oliver Barnham)*

contained details about whom to charge the cost of the trip to.

■ *Meldung über den Kraftfahrunfall*
(Accident Report Form). A detailed form to be completed in the event of an accident.

■ **Handbooks** – Operator's Instruction Manual (*Gerätbeschreibung und Bedienungsanweisung zum Fahrgestell*) and Spare Parts Book (*Ersatzteilliste*)

The driver would also have to maintain several documents specifically relating to running and maintenance. The *Betriebsstofftagebuch* (Daily Fuel Record) recorded details about refuellings and fuel consumption, while the *Kontrollverzeichnis für Werkstattaufträge* (Check List for Shop-repair Orders) gave a record of maintenance and vehicle modifications.

As long as the driver kept all his paperwork filed properly and up to date, he could explain his movements (if stopped and questioned by the Feldgendarmerie, for example), track the maintenance and fuelling of the vehicle and also provide all necessary licence and unit information. Naturally, the chaos of the final months of the war put such diligent administration under strain, but there still appears to be a remarkable degree of order to German paperwork until the very final surrender in May 1945.

Instruments

The Kübelwagen and Schwimmwagen were not especially difficult vehicles to operate. For the Kübelwagen, the dashboard controls and dials were minimal and comprehensible, and mostly contained on a panel section to the right of the driver's wheel. (See the double-page feature 'Kübelwagen operating controls' on pp. 104–05 for more details about the functioning and purpose of each individual control.) The speedometer took central position on the dashboard, and this was framed with four lights, two on each side. To the left, in the upper position, was a red ammeter lamp

LEFT The *Kraftfahrzeugschein* was the primary vehicle registration document that drivers had to carry in any Wehrmacht vehicle. *(Courtesy Oliver Barnham)*

RIGHT The *Fahrnachtweis* or Vehicle Journey Log recorded every journey made by the vehicle. *(Courtesy Oliver Barnham)*

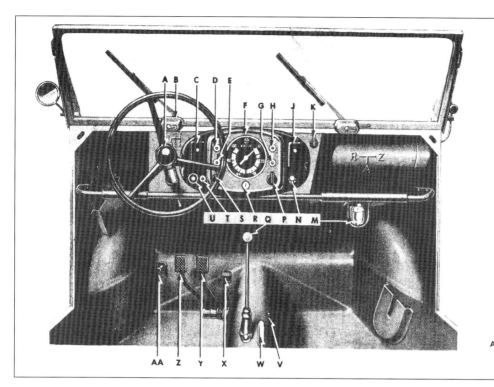

A—HORN BUTTON
B—WINDSHIELD WIPER
C—FUSE BOX
D—AMMETER
E—OIL PRESSURE GAGE
F—SPEEDOMETER
G—BRIGHT LIGHT INDICATOR
H—DIRECTION SIGNAL INDICATOR
J—FUSE BOX
K—DIRECTION SIGNAL SWITCH
L—SPOTLIGHT
M—FUEL COCK
N—MULTIPLE SWITCH
P—LIGHT SWITCH
Q—GEARSHIFT LEVER
R—IGNITION KEY
S—DASHBOARD LIGHT SWITCH
T—TROUBLE LAMP SOCKET
U—CRANKING MOTOR BUTTON
V—CHOKE
W—EMERGENCY BRAKE
X—ACCELERATOR
Y—BRAKE PEDAL
Z—CLUTCH PEDAL
AA—FRONT LIGHT SWITCH

RA PD 322141

ABOVE A diagrammatic breakdown of the Kübelwagen's dashboard, from TM E9-803. Note that later in the war the Kübelwagen was given a far simpler dashboard layout, along the lines of that used in the Schwimmwagen. *(US War Department)*

and below was a green oil pressure lamp; if either of these lamps lit up when the car was above idling speed, it indicated that there was a problem with the generator (or generating system) or oil pressure respectively. The corresponding lamps on the opposite side of the speedometer were the direction signal indicator (at the top) and the headlamp indicator, the latter warning the driver if main lights were turned on when a less visible (to the enemy) mode was more advisable.

Directly beneath the speedometer was the ignition switch, and to the left and right of that were the vehicle's light switches. The left-hand switch operated the dashboard light, while the right switch operated the headlights, tail light and stop light. Moving further outwards on the dashboard there are the vehicle's two fuse boxes set either side of the main control panel. Under the right-hand fuse box was a brown conical Bakelite switch that operated the Notek blackout lights, and on the extreme top right of the control area was the direction signal switch, which would operate both of the indicators depending on which way the switch is flicked.

Looking through the lower right-hand quadrant of the steering wheel, the driver would see two

LEFT The speedometer on a 1942 model Kübelwagen. The red light on the right-hand side is the direction signal indicator and the green light underneath is the headlight indicator. *(Author's collection)*

features on the Kübelwagen – the cranking motor button, necessary to get the motor started (see the description of the starting procedure below), and also an electrical socket into which the occupants of the vehicle could plug a lamp on an extension cord. Controls for the windscreen wipers were integral with the wiper motors, which sat on the bottom rim of the windscreen. The horn button was located directly in the centre of the steering wheel.

Looking beneath the dashboard of the Kübelwagen, we find the main driving controls – gearstick, parking brake, clutch, foot brake and accelerator pedals. A tactically practical addition to the foot pedals was a front light dimmer switch, set to the left of the clutch pedal; this gave the driver the ability to reduce and raise his night lighting according to requirements. To the right-hand side of the parking brake, on the right of the central chassis tunnel, was the vehicle's choke, while underneath the dashboard on the passenger side of the vehicle, was the fuel cock, for shutting off the engine's fuel supply when necessary. One interesting point is that the Type 82 and Type 166 had no fuel gauges, the driver instead using manual dipsticks calibrated to indicate the amount of fuel in the tanks.

As this brief description shows, the Kübelwagen controls were a relatively straightforward affair, making it a simple vehicle to operate. The Schwimmwagen had a more basic layout to the instrument panel, with the controls and indicators being rather less ordered than on the Kübelwagen. The

BELOW Here we see the Kübelwagen's operating pedals. *(Author's collection)*

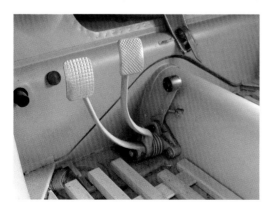

LEFT The Type 166 and Tiger I tank show the relative extremes of the Wehrmacht's vehicle arsenal. The Tiger is from the 1. SS-Panzer-Korps *'Leibstandarte SS Adolf Hitler'*. *(BArch)*

BELOW This image shows SS soldiers deploying in Type 166s in southern France, 1942. The front vehicle has a mounted MG34 to provide immediate defensive fire. *(BArch)*

(As listed in the US War Department Manual TM E9-803.)

a Ignition Switch. The ignition switch is located at the lower center of the instrument panel. A key is furnished to operate the switch. When the key is inserted and turned, the switch serves to close electrical circuits between the battery and ignition coil, direction indicator light, oil pressure light, and dash light switch. All the other circuits are opened and closed by their respective switches.

b Horn Button. The horn button is located in the hub of the steering wheel. When the button is depressed, it closes the circuit between the source of electrical power and the horn, and thus actuates the horn.

c Cranking Motor Button. The cranking motor button is located on the extreme lower left side of the instrument panel. When the cranking motor button is depressed, it closes the electrical circuit between the cranking motor and battery. The cranking motor rotates and, through a series of gears, rotates the engine crankshaft.

d Fuse Boxes. Two rectangular fuse boxes, one at each end, are located on the instrument panel. Most of the electrical circuits in the vehicle pass through one, or the other, of these boxes. In the event a circuit is shorted or overloaded, the fuse burns out. This opens the circuit and prevents damage to any item of equipment, or injury to personnel.

e Trouble Lamp Socket. This socket provides an electrical outlet in which a corded lamp may be plugged, thus providing portable illumination. The socket is located just to the right of the cranking motor button.

f Dash Light Switch. The dash light switch is located on the instrument panel to the right of the trouble lamp socket. When turned on, it closes the circuit between the source of electrical power and the dash light, thus turning on the dash light.

g Light Switch. The light switch is located on the instrument panel just beneath the bright light indicator. When the light switch is turned on it operates the service headlights and service tail and stop light.

h Multiple Switch. The multiple switch is located just to the right of the light switch. The multiple switch has three positions: one 'OFF'; one to turn on the blackout driving light and the blackout tail and stop light; and one to close the circuit to the headlight switch.

i Direction Signal Switch. The direction signal switch is located at the extreme right-hand top side of the instrument panel. It controls the two direction signals located on the outer ends of the windshield. When the switch is turned to the left, the left direction signal is extended, and when the switch is turned to the right, the right direction signal is extended. 'OFF' position of the switch is vertical.

j Fuel Cock. The fuel cock is located at the fuel strainer beneath the fuel tank. Closing the cock shuts off the flow of fuel from the fuel tank to the carburetor on the engine.

k Foot Dimmer Switch. The foot dimmer switch, located on the upward slope of the floor and convenient to the driver's left foot, is used to control the output of the front headlights. Stepping down on the switch operates it.

l Clutch Pedal. The clutch pedal, mounted on a horizontal shaft extending outward from the tunnel in the center of the vehicle, extends upward to a position convenient to the driver's left foot. Depressing the pedal serves to disengage the clutch and thus interrupts the flow of power from the engine to the transmission and driving rear axles. The clutch pedal must be depressed in order to shift gears.

m Brake Pedal. The brake pedal, located just to the right of the clutch pedal, is connected to the mechanical brakes on each wheel through a system of cables. Depressing the brake pedal pulls the cables, which in turn expands the brake shoes within the wheel drums, and slows, or stops the vehicle, depending on the amount of pressure exerted.

n **Accelerator.** The accelerator is located just to the right of the brake pedal. In its released position, the accelerator is adjusted so that the engine will run at idling speed. Depressing the accelerator increases the speed of the engine.

o **Choke.** The choke is mounted to the right of the gearshift lever on the tunnel extending through the center of the vehicle. Pulling out the choke enriches the mixture of gasoline and air being fed from the carburetor into the engine, and thus aids in starting a cold engine.

p **Gearshift Lever.** The gearshift lever, convenient to the driver's right hand, is mounted on the tunnel extending through the center of the vehicle. The lever may be shifted into any of six positions. Five of these are power positions, and one position is neutral. The purpose of the gearshift lever is to provide a means of selecting the proper transmission gear ratio to suit driving conditions.

q **Parking Brake.** In its release position the parking brake lever rests in a horizontal position on the tunnel extending through the center of the vehicle. Pulling up on the parking brake lever operates the same cables as are operated by the service foot brakes, and thus slows or stops the vehicle, depending on the pressure exerted on the brake lever. A toothed segment, on which the lower end of the parking brake is mounted engages a latch on the side of the parking brake lever, providing a means of locking the lever at any position along its arc of travel. This latch is released from the segment by depressing a button in the top of the parking brake lever.

9. INSTRUMENTS.

a **Oil Pressure Gauge.** The oil pressure gage is the lower warning light on the left-hand side of the instrument panel. The light glows green when the ignition is switched on, and is extinguished as soon as the engine is running. If the light glows again after the engine is warmed and running, it indicates the oil pressure has dropped below the safety margin.

b **Ammeter.** The ammeter is the top warning light on the left-hand side of the instrument panel. The light glows red when the ignition is turned on, and is extinguished as soon as the engine is running above its idling speed. If the light should glow while the engine is running above idling speed, it indicates that the generator is not charging, and signifies trouble in the generating circuit.

c **Speedometer.** The speedometer, located in the center of the instrument panel, is graduated in 20 kilometer calibrations from 0 to 100 kilometers. The speedometer indicates the speed at which the vehicle is traveling. A speedometer drive, used to turn speedometer gears, passes through the left front axle.

d **Direction Signal Indicator Light.** The direction signal indicator light is a warning light located at the top right side of the instrument panel. When the direction signal switch is turned, operating either the left or right direction signal, the light flashes on, warning the driver that one of the direction signals is extended. When the switch is turned off, retracting the direction signal, the light flashes off.

e **Bright Light Indicator.** This is a warning light located just beneath the direction signal indicator light. When the headlights are turned on, this indicator light flashes on, and remains on as long as the headlights are in use.

RIGHT A Schwimmwagen stripped of its wheels lies abandoned in a field at the end of the fighting in Normandy. *(Courtesy Alain Roudeix)*

RIGHT The simplicity of the Schwimmwagen dashboard is evident here, especially when compared to the early Kübelwagen. *(Author's collection)*

FAR RIGHT A panel on the Type 166 explains how to engage the gears plus (on the left) low-ratio, high-ratio and four-wheel drive (*Allrad-antrieb*). *(Author's collection)*

RIGHT A restored Schwimmwagen on a film set in France. The aerial at the back is non-standard, but the vehicle colour scheme and other details are correct. *(J. P. Bothorel)*

official Schwimmwagen manual explained the layout thus:

a) Hand and Foot Controls
The foot-pedal cluster incorporates a clutch pedal, brake pedal and throttle pedal. The hand-brake lever, gear lever, four-wheel-drive selector and the carburettor choke control are located on the transmission tunnel. Within easy reach of the driver's hands and feet are the dip switch to the headlights and the operating controls for the central lubrication system and auxiliary fuel pump.

b) Instrument Panel
The instrument panel contains the following equipment: a combined light and ignition switch, starter button, dynamo 'no-charge' warning light, oil pressure warning light, speedometer and trip recorder, fuse box, electric power socket, and panel-light switch. A windscreen wiper motor with its own switch is located on the windshield. The horn button is positioned in the centre of the steering wheel.
(Wehrmacht, 1942, p. 32)

Driving characteristics

Neither the Kübelwagen nor the Schwimmwagen were particularly difficult vehicles to operate, although that is not the same as saying that driving them in combat

conditions was an easy matter. The actual start-up procedure for the Kübelwagen was a fairly intuitive affair, described in detail in the US Kübelwagen manual:

b. Starting Procedure. Turn fuel cock counterclockwise to open. Place gear-shift lever in neutral. Insert ignition key in switch and turn to right, so that ammeter warning light glows red. Depress clutch pedal and pull out choke. Press cranking motor button. Release cranking motor button as soon as the engine starts and push choke half-way in. Permit the engine to run at low speed for two or three minutes to warm up with the choke half-way out. Push the choke all the way in as soon as the engine runs smoothly. If the engine fails to start with the first attempt, repeat the procedure. Do not hold the cranking motor button depressed continuously, for more than ten seconds at a time. Should the engine fail to start after numerous attempts, the carburetor may be flooded. In this circumstance, push the choke all the way in, depress the accelerator, and again attempt to start the engine. If the engine still will not start, refer to the section on trouble shooting.

(US War Department, 1944, p. 12)

Generally speaking, the Kübelwagen and Schwimmwagen were reliable starters, although special techniques might be required to get them going in arctic conditions (see Chapter 6).

Once on the move, both the Kübelwagen and Schwimmwagen had good road holding, exhibiting little of the feared tail-end swing-out on corners that was highlighted by some Allied reviewers, and were capable of up to 80km/h (50mph) on a good surface without obstructions. As already noted, however, the driver could engage a crawler gear for travelling at the same pace as marching infantry, this giving the vehicle a minimum speed of 3km/h (1.8mph). This low gear could also be useful for very slow manoeuvres in off-road terrain, but generally the best gear for arduous cross-country was second, to give a greater range of power when required.

The Kübelwagen's off-road ability lay in a combination of good suspension, excellent traction by virtue of the positive-locking differential, plus a ground clearance of 280mm (11in). With these capabilities it was able to handle a 45% gradient on road conditions and a 40% gradient on a loose sand surface. It could also wade through 450mm (18in) of water without flooding the interior of the vehicle.

BELOW The Type 166 driver's compartment. Note the double magazine rack on the right-hand side for two 50-round *Gurttrommel* drum magazines. Note also the folding handle above the magazine rack. In the upright position this holds the butt of the machine gun. *(Courtesy Oliver Barnham)*

The Kübelwagen and Schwimmwagen were also highly manoeuvrable vehicles, on account of their fairly short wheelbase. The writers of the Humber report carried out a detailed analysis of the captured Kübelwagen's turning circle, and wrote:

The turning circle, ascertained when the vehicle was first received, is 30 ft. 5 ins. on the right-hand lock and 36 ft. 8 ins. on left-hand lock. The left-hand-lock was limited by the steering box stop and the right-hand lock by the tyre fouling against the suspension link. The uneven locks were due to the steering column location in the body, necessitating the steering unit being lined up in an incorrect position on the chassis cross tube. This in turn causes the rocker lever in the steering box to be out of the central position for straight ahead driving. Since neither the body nor the chassis appear to have been damaged to any great extent, it would seem that this is a bad design, especially in view of the absence of locating means for the steering box on the cross tube. It was ascertained that when the steering box is correctly positioned, both locks are limited by the tyres fouling the

suspension links. With the narrower tyres originally specified for the Volkswagen, the locks were restricted by the stops in the steering box, which also is bad practice in view of the fact that thrust loads on full lock are transmitted through the steering box.

(BIOS, 1946, p. 42)

Despite the mechanical restrictions outlined by the engineers, the Kübelwagen's turning circle at least matched, and probably marginally

ABOVE The Trippel Type 2SG/6 amphibious vehicle, which was trialled against the Type 128. It had a six-cylinder engine, four-wheel drive and a five-speed gearbox. *(Courtesy Oliver Barnham)*

LEFT The Schwimmwagens had excellent mobility across mud, and their smooth lower hull could enable them virtually to aquaplane across very deep mud and snow. *(BArch)*

exceeded, that of the Jeep, making it highly manoeuvrable around steep mountain roads or rutted rural tracks. All told, even in the most exacting German field trial reports, there rarely seem to be instances of focused complaint about the Kübelwagen's performance per se. Rather, most of the concerns relate to mechanical problems encountered in several environmental conditions, which we shall look at in more detail later in this chapter and in Chapter 6.

Schwimmwagen – amphibious driving

Looking at the Schwimmwagen specifically, its one great and transparent difference for the driver was that he needed to be confident with amphibious operations. Special training was required – the driver had to know more than just to point his vehicle into a river and drive for the opposite bank. The Schwimmwagen had excellent amphibious characteristics, but it was not to be regarded as a boat. A particularly strong current could spin or carry the light vehicle away with ease, and significant waves could easily lap over the sides into the interior. Furthermore, muddy and steep entry and exit points were real dangers; the worst possible outcome for a Schwimmwagen crew was being stuck fast in river mud directly under the guns of an alerted enemy. Consequently, the Schwimmwagen driver had to make a firm and honest judgement

about whether his vehicle could handle a water obstacle before his wheels began rolling down the bank.

As part of his training, the Schwimmwagen driver would be taught to assess the speed of a river current before entering the water. The speed of current not only affected the safety of the vehicle, but it also had implications for the point at which the driver entered the water – faster currents would produce more downriver drift, so the faster currents required a higher upstream entry point to put the car at a chosen exit point. The official manual lists four types of water-current classification: 1) below 1m/s as weak current; 2) between 1 and 1.5m/s as medium current; 3) between 1.5 and 2.5m/s as strong current; 4) above 2.5m/s as very strong current.

As a general rule, the driver would want to avoid crossing waterways that exhibited strong or very strong current levels, although the emergencies of war might demand so. The manual explains the point that 'It is not possible to progress against a current which exceeds 2.5 m/s, and under these conditions, the vehicle should first be driven an appropriate distance up-river and, once in the water, the bow kept pointing upstream in order to lessen the drift' (Wehrmacht, 1942, p. 47). An interesting note in the manual also recommends that prior to entering the water the driver and any occupants swap their steel helmets for field caps, just in case the troops find themselves in the water and have to swim for safety.

THIS PAGE In this series of photographs, a German Schwimmwagen crew conducts amphibious practice in a French canal. Note the cooperation between the driver and the individual deploying the propeller unit. *(BArch)*

LEFT A rear view of the Type 128. Note the position of the twin exhaust pipes, and the plug covering the dog clutch on the propeller housing. These features were both changed in the Type 166. *(Courtesy of the Porsche Archive)*

In preparation for an amphibious action, the driver would first reconnoitre the river bank to choose suitable places for entry and egress – ideally shallow slopes of firm ground, such as shingle or solid earth, and free of any obstacles that might cause serious damage to the propeller and its housing. The maximum angle of entry into the water was about 40 degrees. The driver would also have to ensure that any loads within the vehicle – people, weapons or cargo – were evenly distributed inside, with no gross imbalances of weight that might cause the vehicle to list or otherwise affect its handling in the water. He would also raise the windscreen to serve as a basic splash protector. Prior to entering the water, the safety strap connected to the propeller assembly was disconnected and stowed for transit through an attachment on the engine cover.

The manual goes on to explain the actual entry and driving method:

> *Engage cross-country gear, or four-wheel-drive and first gear, depending on shore conditions. Enter the water slowly and if possible at a near-horizontal attitude to avoid water entering the vehicle. The wheels will continue to touch the bottom until the craft floats freely. When it is in motion, use the front wheels to steer.*
>
> *Disengage cross-country gear and put the main gearbox in neutral. Leave the four-wheel-drive selector in the middle position while the vehicle is in the water.*

CENTRE A VW prototype amphibian during early trials. *(Courtesy Oliver Barnham)*

LEFT This view of the Type 128 trials gives an excellent impression of the off-road mobility achieved by the vehicle's four-wheel drive. *(Courtesy of the Porsche Archive)*

With the motor running at tick-over speed, lower the propeller assembly, using the handling-rod provided for the purpose. Do not attempt to connect the propeller when the engine is running fast.

Engine speed can be increased as soon as the propeller has engaged. If the propeller hits an obstacle and disengages, slow down at once to enable it to reconnect.

On water, as on land, steering is performed by moving the front wheels, which act as rudders.

(Wehrmacht, 1942, p. 47)

The Schwimmwagen had good amphibious characteristics, but this is not to say that the journey across a wide river was comfortable. Choppy water could and did slop over the sides, soaking the occupants, and spray could be constant. The biggest threat, of course, was from the enemy catching the Schwimmwagen on water, and holing the hull with gunfire. That problem had to be addressed by wider tactical measures, such as supporting fire from the friendly bank or good reconnaissance to find uncontested crossings. Another danger was propeller failure, either through mechanical fault or through striking an underwater object. In fact, the vehicle could actually still make way through the water if the propeller failed completely; the driver would engage the four-wheel-drive and third gear, and the action of the tyres turning through the water kept the vehicle going forward at a moderate speed. The vehicle was also equipped as standard

ABOVE Given the dangling foliage and weed, this Schwimmwagen has evidently just crossed water. For anti-armour protection, the crew carry a Panzerfaust at the ready. *(Courtesy Oliver Barnham)*

with oars and a boat pole, which could be used to assist steering, give extra power or help get the vehicle moving again if it was stuck on soft ground. One further point to note is that if the driver needed to make his vehicle go backwards in the water, via the oars or

BELOW Soldiers from the *Grossdeutschland* Division are here seen making an amphibious crossing. The water level rises high up the vehicles, particularly the vehicle in the background, which is experiencing more wash. *(BArch)*

with the land and the vehicle could drive away normally. As the driver moved off, he was advised to apply the brakes several times repeatedly to dry out the brake linings, and he would also pump the handle of the central lubrication system, using the oil to force out any water from lubrication points.

Driving experience

The amphibious handling of the Schwimmwagen was a very specific technical and tactical challenge. What can we say, however, about the broader experience of handling these vehicles during wartime?

ABOVE A German Army Schwimmwagen unit forms a small convoy in Italy. *(Courtesy Oliver Barnham)*

poles, the propeller assembly would need to be lifted out of the water first.

Exiting the water could be a particularly tricky business for the driver, especially in strong current conditions, as the rear of the vehicle would swing around dramatically as the front wheels reconnected with the land. The driver's assistant had to be ready with the handling rod connected to the propeller housing, prepared to raise the housing up quickly to the stowed position if it was threatened with damage, and when all four wheels were eventually engaged

BELOW A Type 166 on the Eastern Front. Spare fuel cans are strapped to the front hull, and note the standard Kübelwagen tyres, without snow chains. *(Courtesy Oliver Barnham)*

GERMAN LIGHT VEHICLES

The Kübelwagen and Schwimmwagen worked alongside numerous other German light vehicles throughout the war. During the 1930s, the German armed services relied heavily on adaptations of commercial vehicles for military use, which resulted in wide variations amongst units. From 1934, greater order to this system was attempted through a vehicular classification system, which arranged vehicles according to their tactical and physical capabilities. The Kübelwagen fell into the *leichter Personenkraftwagen* (l.Pkw/ Light Personnel Vehicle) class, as did many other vehicles, and each vehicle was given a *Kraftfahrzeug* (Kfz) number. The other vehicles in the l.Pkw class were built by Hanomag, BMW and Stöwer. A good example of such a vehicle is the Kfz 2 (Stöwer 40). This had an AW2 or R180W water-cooled four-cylinder engine and four-wheel drive, with five forward and one reverse gears. Unlike the Kübelwagen, the engine was front mounted. The chassis was the standard type for a light military car, of a rectangular frame of rectangular section with bracing to support the engine, transmission and body. Performance of all the l.Pkw vehicles was generally inferior to that of the Kübelwagen, and the Porsche vehicle was typically the vehicle of choice for those wanting the best cross-country performance, despite the fact that the Kübelwagen was not four-wheel drive.

Making statements about the general experience of driving the Kübelwagen is precarious. As any car owner knows, one man's meat can truly be another man's poison, and while one individual might class the Kübelwagen as his transport of choice, another might regard it as a vehicle to be avoided at all costs, depending upon experience. Also, we have to remember that Kübelwagens and Schwimmwagens were hard-used operational vehicles. With punishing use and extended mileage, each vehicle acquires its own set of problems and peculiarities, so we must be cautious about applying inductive reasoning, generalising about what it was like to drive *all* Kübelwagens because of the experience of what it was like to drive one of them. Driving modern restored vehicles, while giving a useful impression of their performance and occupant experience, is not a complete solution either, not least because the owners of these expensive and rare vehicles are rarely willing to subject them to the type of brutal driving that they would have had during the war years.

As we have seen in this book already, there are several insightful English-language evaluations of wartime driving, and as always once we have peeled away the propaganda bias there are some useful nuggets of information about driving experience. For example, British war correspondent John Dugdale, writing for *Autocar* in October 1941, put a captured Kübelwagen through its paces and came to the following conclusions:

As to performance, this is livelier than previous reports had indicated, the get-away being particularly snappy. The engine, which has previously been described as rough by British standards, is naturally not as smooth as the usual six [cylinder engine], but it must be admitted that what roughness there is is counterbalanced by the rear engine mounting, by means of which the sounds and odours of a struggling motor are placed conveniently behind one. How tempting it must be to overdrive a rear-engined car with the protest of the over-stressed engine wafted away unheeded behind.

Considering the distance from pedals to engine, the controls were positive, but this particular clutch was fierce. The gear lever

was noticeably positive, and must have an excellent remote control.

In spite of four-wheel independent suspension, the springing was not so outstanding as might have been expected, but then the desert, with its multitude of small rocks and hillocks, is the worst surface in the world.

(Dugdale, *Autocar*, 17 October 1941)

Coming from an Allied pen so early in the war, this review is remarkably even-handed in its judgements, and finds much to praise in the Kübelwagen's handling and performance. In particular, he notes the positive if occasionally heavy experience of the controls. Interestingly, Dugdale feels that the suspension doesn't quite

ABOVE Soldiers from the Panzergrenadier Division *Grossdeutschland* scan the skies for enemy aircraft. Interestingly, all the occupants are armed with MP44 weapons – history's first true assault rifle. *(BArch)*

BELOW This evocative image from the Type 166 trials shows the vehicle nimbly negotiating a German woodland. *(Porsche Museum)*

ABOVE The MG34 was better suited to vehicle mounts, but here these Type 166s have the faster-firing MG42 on the front mount.
(Courtesy Oliver Barnham)

deliver on its promise, but accepts that a lack of comfort is inevitable given the terrain.

Another Brit who took to the wheel of a captured Kübelwagen was an officer in the Royal Electrical and Mechanical Engineers (REME) – known just as 'Recce' – who took one on a 5,000km adventure through Italy and Sicily between July 1943 and June 1944, writing up his experiences for that content-hungry publication, *Autocar*. The most revealing part of this entertaining account comes from an extremely arduous off-road section of the journey:

> *For the first 10 miles we have a very dull time with slow convoys. This delay was bad, but at dusk we caught the tail of another large convoy which was entering Carlini. The 1/25,000 map showed a cart track which by-passed Carlini and Lentini, joining the Catania road beyond Lentini. We tried it. The track quickly deteriorated, until we found ourselves slithering down a precipitous slope where scorched cart wheels had worn two ruts some 8 ins. wide and 18 ins. deep. I stopped the car on a slightly more gradual gradient, and we scotched the wheels with rocks. Then I tried to change into reverse,*

LEFT A Kübelwagen wheel change. It appears that the official jack has been lost, as the vehicle is blocked up on a fuel can. *(BArch)*

but found I could not move the gear from second. The gearbox being absolutely inaccessible, as previously indicated, it was impossible to take the lid off and sort out the gears. By moving five yards at a time, however, and building a road of sorts in front, we eventually covered some three miles in six hours and reached the bottom without incurring any serious damage.

The next 20 miles to the leaguer above Primasole bridge was performed slowly, in second gear. Owing to the constant dread of overheating we arrived at dawn, tired out. Later a jeep tried this track and I had the pleasure of seeing it recovered on a direct lift. It had both front shock absorbers and one front spring smashed. This had been the only occasion on which the Volkswagen let me down in some 5,000 kiloms. on the island and in Italy. Long may it continue to serve the Allied cause so faithfully.

('Recce', *Autocar*, 7 June 1944)

This account is useful not only for giving a sense of the Kübelwagen's impressive durability, but also for what it says about the driving experience. Regarding the former, even notwithstanding the gear failure, the fact

ABOVE This wartime image gives a realistic impression of what the interior of a combat vehicle is like. Items inside include the *Zeltbahn* shelter-half, water bottles and coats. *(Courtesy Oliver Barnham)*

remains that the Kübelwagen handled terrain that totally incapacitated a Jeep, the US vehicle possibly being more vulnerable to suspension impact damage because of its greater weight.

By far the most useful observations about the experience of driving the Kübelwagen,

BELOW A camouflaged Type 166 conducts an amphibious test run along a canal in Normandy. *(Courtesy Oliver Barnham)*

however, come from the detailed post-trial and post-deployment reports compiled by the Germans over the war years. What is notable about them is that, by and large, the reports don't list the actual core design or performance of the vehicle as problematic. This does not simply seem a case of officialdom avoiding the issue. In fact, the reports are often exhaustively compiled and unsparing in listing the problems encountered by the vehicles during the period of assessment. But there appear to be no back-to-the-drawing-board moments, just a large collection of incremental improvements and recommendations such as would be experienced by any military vehicle in the field. The millions of Reichsmarks and countless hours of testing and improvement during the war paid off.

BELOW A test run of the Type 166, conducted by Porsche in the mountains near Salzburg. *(Porsche Museum)*

Extreme conditions

This book is not the place for a detailed study of general German driving skills in every theatre of the war. Yet while in Chapter 6 we will look in detail at the myriad mechanical issues to which drivers and mechanics had to attend on the Kübelwagen and Schwimmwagen, it is worth briefly outlining some of the regular non-mechanical challenges faced by drivers in some of the most demanding theatres. In North Africa, for example, drivers obviously had to contend with the extreme heat – both its effects on them and on the vehicles – and the all-pervading dust. Much of the driver's time would actually be spent on maintenance, just to keep the vehicle running. The material expansions and contractions from heat and the direct sunshine could cause significant damage to any components made from wood, plastic, leather, rubber or cloth, so these would need to be checked regularly and repaired or replaced as necessary. Tyre pressures might need frequent adjustment to compensate for the rapid increase in ground temperature throughout the day, although it was not advised running them at below the prescribed pressures. An official report noted that the driver should check his tyre pressure an hour after beginning a journey, and at four-hourly intervals thereafter, monitoring that the pressures don't drop below their officially stated levels. For travel across very loose sand, the Kübelwagen could be fitted with smooth wide sand tyres, to improve cross-country mobility.

Dust ingress into mechanical parts was by far the worst problem faced by Kübelwagen crews in North Africa. The specifics of dealing with dust issues are explored in more detail in Chapter 6, but suffice to say that the driver would spend many hours a day coping with the pervasive effects of tiny particles. (The Humber report Kübelwagen, when inspected by the British engineers, was found to be carrying 45kg/100lb of sand and dust particles in its frame). A dust storm would bring an entire German column to a halt.

The harshness of the desert terrain required

Kübelwagen drivers to gain experience and exhibit a cautious logic. Everything was different to the temperate zones in which they had likely trained. Even the vehicle's performance was affected – the lower air pressure in tropical climates meant that the engine received less air than normal, which in turn had the effect of raising fuel consumption. Navigation was problematic in seemingly featureless expanses, and when driving in column it was hard to maintain correct course and distance because of the dust kicked up by the vehicle in front, even with the Notek lights engaged. It was recommended that long marches were punctuated by regular pauses, in which the vehicles would ideally be parked in the wind with their hoods opened, to allow the movement of air to both cool and clean the vehicle. Conversely, when the vehicles were parked, they also had to be protected from direct sunlight, further dust ingress and the possibilities of enemy attack. Exhaust pipes would be fitted with plugs, and tyres and other rubber components were covered with sheets. Camouflage could be applied via netting or by the judicious use of vegetation (of which there was little). For longer stops, the crew might dig a large vehicle trench or make a protective structure from rocks, to provide a shield from small-arms fire and shell splinters.

On any operation, the driver had to ensure that he and all his occupants had adequate drinking water to sustain them throughout the duration of a journey.

Travelling in the early morning or the late evening were the preferred options, not only because the heat was more bearable but also because there was a reduced danger of being spotted by an enemy fighter-bomber and strafed up. The basis of desert driving was to keep a steady pace in a higher gear, avoiding the sudden accelerations that could cause wheelspin and a stuck vehicle. The speed of movement, however, depended squarely on the type of terrain encountered, and in this regard North Africa offered a surprising variety. The ground included sand deserts, stone deserts, salt pans, gravel flats and glutinous swamps. The drivers had to familiarise themselves with driving across all these surfaces, and they became bitterly

acquainted with the effect of each on their vehicles. In deep, soft sand, for example, even a light and nimble vehicle such as the Kübelwagen could become stuck, and had to be released via a combination of digging out and the correct use of sand boards. Simply thrashing the engine mercilessly in an attempt to get free could result in a broken powertrain. In hard, rocky desert areas, there were two primary problems. The first was damage to tyres inflicted by constant rubbing contact with sharp, hot rocks. The second was twisting and impact damage imparted to the vehicle's body panels, mountings, suspension and shock absorbers – drivers were advised to study the terrain ahead closely before driving off, to plan the least demanding route for both vehicle and crew.

BELOW Tunisia, 1943. Following heavy rains, a Kübelwagen driver wrestles to gain traction in glutinous mud. Note how the mud adheres to the smooth sand tyres. *(BArch)*

BOTTOM A view of the front passenger side of the Kübelwagen, showing the windscreen wiper motor and side direction indicator. *(Author's collection)*

GERMAN ARMY ADVICE TO DESERT DRIVERS

The following advice was given to German drivers operating in Libya in 1942, via a manual entitled *The Soldier in Libya*. The translation was done by the US Military Intelligence Service and published in their *Intelligence Bulletin*:

Because of the high temperature of the surrounding air and the high engine temperature, part of your fuel will evaporate. In addition, more fuel will be used on all the roads, with the exception of the good coastal highways and a few other tarred routes, because the roads are merely trails. The fuel consumption is increased by about one-fourth of the usual amount, and you must take along some reserve cans.

For fuel we generally use gasoline with an octane content of 76. In this hot region the gasoline which we now use with an octane content of 74 will cause the engine to knock. If in exceptional cases we are given gasoline with an octane content that is lower than 76, we should mix with it some motor oil so as to increase its knock-resistance (to 10 quarts of fuel with an octane content of 74 and below, add about 1 quart of motor oil).

A special motor oil, the lubricating power and viscosity of which are suitable for tropical temperatures, is issued. If in special cases another oil must be put in, the driver first must see whether or not the new oil will mix with the kind he is already using. Many oils cannot be mixed and lead to saponification (changing into soap), thus destroying the lubricating power. If the oils will not mix, we must let out all the oil we have, wash out the motor housing with 1 or 2 quarts of oil, empty it again, and then fill it with new oil. Continuing the trip, we must observe the oil-pressure gauge carefully. If the pressure drops below one atmosphere, we should stop. The engine must cool off for a time. If the driver continues with an oil

pressure below one atmosphere in spite of this condition, there is danger of wearing out the bearings.

Openings for oil, air exhausts, and air filters should be provided with special filters (wet filters) to prevent entrance of the fine desert sand which is blowing continually. When we fill up with water, fuel, and oil, and when we grease the vehicle, we must clean the openings and the lubricating places carefully and remove all sand. We should pay special attention to the care of the filter. Each time we tank up, we should take out the wet filter, wash it with gasoline or kerosene, and then soak it again with motor oil; in the case of other types, we should set the filter in the oil bath that is provided. When we take out the filter, we should cover the open filter housing with a rag so that no sand may get in it while it is open; otherwise, this fine, sharp-grained sand will destroy the vehicle in a short time. Because of all of the moving parts, the sand acts like fine sandpaper. The temperature range from day to night is often over 30°. If a vehicle has been running in the daytime and is allowed to stand and cool at night, dew may gather on it, and, in addition to the rust danger, this may also lead to serious and time-robbing ignition disturbances. In the morning, if the engine does not start at once, further attempts to start it are useless (the batteries may run down). We must see whether a spark passes on the spark plugs. If not, we should search all the cable connections of the ignition, the ignition distributors, and other movable parts of the ignition for a ground due to water. We should not try to start until we have dried all the wet parts.

A vital part of the vehicle is the battery; we should not fail to take care of it. Because of the hot climate of this region, and the heat that is radiated from the engine, the distilled water of a battery is evaporated very quickly. *Examine the battery every day to see whether or not the liquid stands about ½ inch above the plates. If the water is too low, pour in distilled water. In case of emergency, we may also use boiled water.*

Apart from the first-class highways of Libya, many roads and trails have a relatively hard, thin surface. Under this is loose sand. In order to lessen sinking in as much as possible, we should use the following methods:

The pressure in the tires, insofar as the load of the vehicle will permit, should be decreased so that the tires will have a maximum bearing surface.

Don't make any sharp movements of the wheel, don't throw on the brakes violently, and don't run backward. In doing these things, we can easily break through the surface layer and cause the vehicle to sink in. If, beforehand, we recognize a place as a soft stretch of sand, we cross it on a rope ladder or on a wire net if we cannot go around it.

If the vehicle has sunk in, don't try to go either backwards or forwards by giving gas, because we will accomplish nothing in this way; we should stop the engine, lift the vehicle with the jack and put under the sunken wheel the planks that we have brought along with us. After we have lifted the vehicle, we should put sand in the hole caused by the sinking in of the wheel so that the plank will have a good surface to rest on. Of course we should also put a board under the jack; otherwise, the vehicle will not be lifted and the jack will sink in the soft sand. After we have put the wheel on the plank, we should then start the motor and drive out with as little gas and as little turning of the wheel as possible (don't forget to pick up the tools).

(US Military Intelligence Service, 1942)

LEFT The choke, gearstick and the handbrake on the Kübelwagen. The handbrake lever was known to be easily broken by a heavy hand. *(Author's collection)*

At the opposite extreme to the North African landscapes, the drivers of Kübelwagens and Schwimmwagens also had to contend with the grim daily realities of driving on the Eastern Front. Although the cruel Russian winter most readily springs to mind when we think of vehicular problems on the Eastern Front, actually the Soviet Union presented the drivers with all manner of terrain and environment challenges. During the hot summer months, the Russian and Ukrainian steppes could be reminiscent of North African deserts, being extremely dusty and rocky, with high daytime temperatures and plenty of direct, baking sunlight. The driver's workload intensified, however, during the terrible seasonal rains, concentrated in the spring and

BELOW Rubber and fabric parts of the vehicle were particularly vulnerable to mildew, insect damage and general environmental wear and tear. *(Author's collection)*

the autumn. Depending on the type of soil, these rains could turn previously passable tracks and roads into horrendous quagmires of glutinous mud. The translation of a German 1942 manual on winter warfare, *Taschenbuch für den Winterkrieg* (5 August 1942), was realistic about these conditions:

Light soil, especially sand, permits water to drain off, but the dark humus of the Ukraine turns into well-nigh untraversable, sticky mud. Wheeled and tracked vehicles are unable to use paved roads and highways, while the ground is mired. ... Wheeled motor vehicles should be prohibited on muddy roads, and tracked vehicles should only be employed in emergencies. Heavy wheeled vehicles or sleds should be replaced by light carts, high two-wheeled vehicles, boat sleds, or pack animals.

(US Military Intelligence Service, 1943, p. 3)

From photographic evidence, it is clear that wheeled and tracked vehicles continued to struggle through the deep muds, contra the official advice. The Kübelwagen and Schwimmwagen would perform better than many other vehicles in the German inventory, but the drivers would still have a hard time preventing the vehicles from sliding or from grinding to a halt with mud wrapped around the wheels and axles. (The Schwimmwagen would have the advantage of its smooth lower hull forming a glide surface over the mud.) A different type of problem would occur with the onset of the first freezes of winter (from October onwards, depending on the location in the Soviet Union). At this stage, the deeply rutted tracks would harden, forming sharp ridges that could immobilise a vehicle with all the efficiency of a tank trap. Again, photographs show Kübelwagens stuck fast on such hardened ruts, the power wheels suspended helplessly in mid-air. Often the best course of action for a Kübelwagen or Schwimmwagen driver might be to tap into the vehicle's off-road performance and attempt movement through virgin land, rather than well-worn tracks.

Of course, the ultimate test for Kübelwagen or Schwimmwagen crews was the Soviet winter. The first, exceptionally cruel winter of 1941/42 taught the Wehrmacht some sharp lessons about vehicle maintenance in arctic conditions, especially about fuel/oil composition and the requirements for vehicle warming before starting. With the onset of the snows and sub-zero temperatures, the Kübelwagen driver would have to ensure that his vehicle was properly winterised. Snow-chains had to be fitted to all tyres, and at temperatures below -20°C (-4°F) the motor oil had to be thinned with 15% petrol and 25% petrol at anything below -30°C. The driver or any assigned mechanic would also have to monitor the dilution levels constantly, as the petrol would steadily evaporate as the engine was run.

Both the Kübelwagen and the Schwimmwagen had the distinct advantage of being air-cooled vehicles, which meant that they avoided the problems of frozen coolant fluid. Yet starting the vehicles could still be a fraught business in extremely low temperatures. For a start, moving and vulnerable parts had to be kept as free from snow and ice as possible. If viable, the vehicle was parked on ground sheets

or fir tree bows, to provide some insulation, and a camouflaged sheet thrown over the entire vehicle was a good protective move. Battery power was severely weakened by the cold, so oil lamps were used to bring the batteries up to an operating temperature. When it came to the actual starting procedure, the Schwimmwagen manual offered the following advice, which was also relevant for the Kübelwagen:

In cold weather, before switching on the ignition, turn the engine over about twenty times using the starting-handle. Then, with the ignition 'On' but without touching the accelerator, use the electric starter. If the engine fails to fire, get a second person to hand-crank the motor whilst pressing the starter button. In this way the weakened battery will be spared and the spark will be stronger. Continue this joint starting effort for at least one minute.

(Wehrmacht, 1942, p. 39)

If this procedure did not work, or temperatures had dropped below -30°C (-22°F), then the crew had to resort to the vehicle's cold-weather starting kit, which gave the

LEFT As an experimental measure to increase snow mobility, this Kübelwagen has been fitted with double rear wheels and front and back snow chains. *(Courtesy of the Porsche Archive)*

option of starting the engine on high-octane fuel sent straight to the carburettor. The Schwimmwagen manual again clarifies:

… pour approximately half a litre of priming fuel into the starting-fuel container, and switch the two-way tap on top of the fuel pump to draw from this auxiliary tank. Try starting the engine again and if it runs, switch the tap back to the main tank. If the engine fails to fire, shut off the tap. If the engine stops after running for only a short time, it is probable that not enough priming fuel was used to sufficiently warm the engine to enable it to operate on normal fuel. This may easily occur at temperatures below minus 30 degrees C. In this situation, repeat attempts to start with high-octane priming fuel.

(Wehrmacht, 1942, p. 40).

Actually starting the vehicle was just the beginning of the ordeal for the winter driver. The driver would then have to negotiate snowdrifts, patches of glassy ice, hidden drops and frozen lakes. As with driving over soft sand, it was best if the driver could maintain a constant speed and evenly applied traction when crossing snowy land. If traversing iced-over rivers,

BELOW An early model Type 166 from the rear. Compared to the Type 128, the exhaust pipes have now moved to the top of the vehicle. The drop-down rear reflector was later omitted. *(Courtesy Oliver Barnham)*

LEFT This Type 166 belongs to the *Grossdeutschland* Division, as indicated by the white helmet painted on the side. The other symbol indicates that the division has half-track motorisation. *(Courtesy Oliver Barnham)*

extreme care was required. A Kübelwagen or Schwimmwagen largely needed ice of 152mm (6in) thickness to be assured a safe crossing in column of march, alongside horse and infantry. Ice over still water could support heavier loads than ice over flowing water.

The driver's burden

In this chapter, we have mostly looked at the environmental challenges of manning a Kübelwagen or Schwimmwagen. Layered on top of this, as we saw in Chapter 4, would be the numerous responsibilities of general soldiering which the driver would have to fulfil. It is one thing to perform hours of cross-country driving, but another thing entirely to do the same driving under wartime conditions, with scant hours of sleep, terrible and real dangers surrounding you, and personal participation in violent action. The Wehrmacht's reputation as one of the world's most professional military forces to a large extent depended upon many thousands of drivers, who kept the war machine mobile and equipped. Driving a Kübelwagen or Schwimmwagen would have been a very different experience to, say, driving a truck, half-track or tank. All front-line drivers, however, would have exhibited the same endurance and fortitude as any other soldier in the Third Reich.

RIGHT Luftwaffe and Kriegsmarine personnel sit in their Kübelwagen in Sicily, 1943. With the windscreen folded, both wiper motors stand out clearly on the frame. *(BArch)*

Chapter Six

The engineer's view

The Kübelwagen and Schwimmwagen were not, comparatively, complicated vehicles to maintain. They were reliable and tough, and so in moderate operational conditions with regular levels of servicing and repair they could be generally kept going without onerous manpower hours.

OPPOSITE A group of army personnel receive training in the mechanics of the Schwimmwagen's engine and propeller unit. *(Courtesy Oliver Barnham)*

ABOVE This photograph gives an excellent impression of the conditions within a field workshop. Note the smashed-out windscreen on the Kübelwagen. *(BArch)*

As we have seen so far in this book, the Kübelwagen and Schwimmwagen were frequently put through the most extreme mechanical experiences, their engines, gearboxes and drive trains overstressed and their bodies pounded by tortured landscapes. Thus, the mechanically minded driver and the

mechanics of the *Heeres Kraft Parks* (Vehicle Repair Stations) and divisional transport service centres would have been called upon to deliver every conceivable type of repair and remedy, often conducted from an improvised repair shop, such as a shattered hut in a Ukrainian village or a hastily erected tent to shield from the Italian winter rains.

This chapter looks at the general maintenance requirements of the Kübelwagen and Schwimmwagen under operational conditions, and examines the physical problems (and remedies) that revealed themselves in war. What it shows is that neither the Kübelwagen nor the Schwimmwagen were invulnerable, and needed the attention of diligent hands to keep them running.

Operational maintenance

As with any other vehicle in the German arsenal, the Kübelwagen and Schwimmwagen depended upon a predictable schedule of servicing and maintenance to keep them in the best running order. In terms of distance-specific servicing, the schedule roughly broke down as follows (based on recommendations in D662/13):

Distance in km	Task
1,000	• Check battery levels and terminals • Check tyre pressures
1,500	• Check fan-belt tension
2,000	• Clean spark plugs • Renew oil in oil-bath air filter • Fill central lubrication system (Schwimmwagen)
3,000	• Check wheel bearings for play • Clean fuel-oil filter
5,000	• Clean distributor points • Replenish oil in rear shock absorbers
6,000	• Check valves for excessive play
10,000	• Repack wheel bearings with grease

In addition to the above, it was recommended that the vehicle be lubricated whenever it was cleaned.

RIGHT Two soldiers put together signposts on the bonnet of their Schwimmwagen. The car horn is the late-war Bakelite version. *(BArch)*

ENGINE TUNE-UP PROCEDURE

Advice on tuning up the engine from TM E9-803:

a. *Spark Plugs. Remove and clean spark plugs. Examine the plug for cracked porcelain; adjust the gap with an 0.025-inch wire gage.*

b. *Battery and Ignition Cables. Inspect the ground strap and cranking motor cable to see that connections are clean and tight and free of corrosion; cover the connections with a thin layer of grease. The battery is located in the left rear of the vehicle, forward of the engine compartment. The cranking motor is mounted on the right hand side of the differential housing. Check the primary ignition system for clean and tight connections.*

c. *Distributor. Inspect distributor points for evidence of pitting or burning. If not too badly pitted or burned, points may be filed as a method of emergency repair. When points are badly pitted or burned, replace. To adjust the contact points, turn the distributor shaft until the fiber rubbing block of the breaker arm is exactly on high point of the cam lobe. Adjust the gap between faces of adjustable point and contact arm point to 0.020-inch clearance by loosening the lock screw and turning the eccentric adjusting screw until proper clearance is obtained. Tighten the adjustable point lock screw and recheck the gap.*

d. *Carburetor. Remove and clean the oil-bath air cleaner and refill with clean oil to the proper level. Check the carburetor and gasoline line for leaks. No adjustment other than idling speed is provided. With engine warm, turn idler adjusting screw, out to enrich the mixture, in to lean the mixture.*

(War Department, 1944, p. 64)

In addition to the regular servicing events in a vehicle's life, the Kübelwagen and Schwimmwagen needed day-to-day attention to keep everything in order, particularly during periods of hard operational use. The US War Department's Kübelwagen manual is a useful English-language source for these procedures. It breaks down the in-field servicing requirements into three main areas: 'Before operation', 'During operation' and 'At-halt' (i.e. post-journey). Given the logical nature of its descriptions, these categories were also relevant for German maintenance procedures.

The purpose of the 'Before operation service'

LEFT AND BELOW
A Kübelwagen tool kit, which was stowed in a designated area in the right side of the engine compartment. *(Author's collection)*

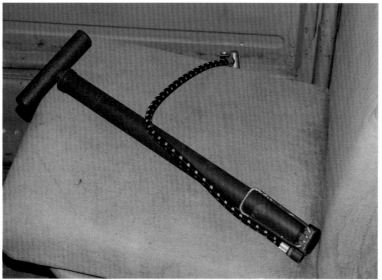

decelerate engine a few times and listen for any unusual vibration or noise' (War Department, 1944, p. 27). The driver also needed to check electrical functions, such as lights and windscreen wipers.

The manual's extensive list of checks would have become second nature to well-trained combat drivers and mechanics, equivalent to the way a professional soldier automatically checks his firearm before heading into action.

The 'During operation service' was basically an exercise in paying attention to the vehicle in transit, and noting anything out of the ordinary that might require mechanical attention either immediately or at halt.

> *While vehicle is in motion, listen for such sounds as rattles, knocks, squeals, or hums that may indicate trouble. Look for indications of trouble in air cooling system and smoke from any part of the vehicle. Be on the alert to detect any odor of overheating components or units such as generator, brakes, or clutch; fuel vapor from a leak in fuel system, exhaust gas, or other signs of trouble. Each time the brakes are used, gears shifted, or vehicle turned, consider this a test, and notice any unsatisfactory or unusual instrument indications that may signify possible trouble in the system to which the instrument pertains.*
>
> (War Department, 1944, p. 27)

The operator was urged to be especially sensitive to noises or troubles with the brakes, suspension, shock absorbers and, naturally, the engine. These were not just general mechanical concerns. Failure of one of these components could result in the occupants of the vehicle being stranded under enemy fire or even trapped behind enemy lines; a broken-down vehicle was as dangerous for a soldier as a malfunctioning firearm.

The 'At-halt service' was critical to the continuing reliability of the vehicle. This maintenance step was not just a matter of repairing any damage or issues, but also of implementing the preventative measures to guard against future problems. The importance of a thorough At-halt service is such that it is worth quoting from the manual in full:

TOP The 6-volt Bosch windscreen wiper motor, as fitted on both the Kübelwagen and the Schwimmwagen. The on/off switch sits on the top. *(Author's collection)*

ABOVE A standard-issue vehicle tyre pump. The Kübelwagen's tyre pressures were 20.5psi at the front, and 26.5psi at the rear. *(Author's collection)*

is basically to ensure that the vehicle is in a sound condition to perform its duties, the mechanic checking for any signs of damage or sabotage prior to driving. In many ways it is similar to vehicle roadworthiness tests performed on civilian vehicles today, with some added investigations to prepare for combat duties. The engineers recommended checking all external parts, including bodywork, tyres and stowed tools and equipment. In addition, the vehicle's fuel and oil levels needed to be measured, and the engine turned over: 'With the engine running above idling speed, red light (ammeter) and green light (oil pressure) must go out. If either light burns, stop engine and investigate or report trouble. Accelerate and

23. AT-HALT SERVICE.

a. *Importance.* The At-halt Service may be regarded as minimum battle maintenance and should be performed under all tactical conditions, even though more extensive maintenance services must be slighted or omitted altogether.

b. *Procedures.* At-halt Service consists of investigating any deficiencies noted during operation, inspecting items listed below according to the procedures following the items, and correcting any deficiencies found. Deficiencies not corrected should be reported promptly to the designated individual in authority.

(1) *ITEM 38, FUEL AND OIL.* Check to see that there is adequate fuel and engine oil to operate to next scheduled stop. Replenish supply if needed.

(2) *ITEM 39, TEMPERATURES, HUBS, BRAKE DRUMS, TRANSMISSION, AND AXLE.* Hand-feel wheel hubs, brake drums, transmission, differential, and rear wheel final reduction gear housing for abnormal temperatures.

(3) *ITEM 42, SUSPENSION.* Inspect torsion arms, traverse spring housings, and center housings for damage and loose mountings. Inspect shock absorbers for loose mountings and worn linkage. Check front axle to front frame head for secure mounting.

(4) *ITEM 43, STEERING LINKAGE.* Inspect Pitman arm and linkage for looseness or damage.

(5) *ITEM 44, WHEEL STUD NUTS.* Inspect all wheel stud nuts to see that they are present and secure. See that hub caps are securely mounted.

(6) *ITEM 45, TIRES.* Inspect for flats or low pressure, missing valve caps, cuts, and bruises. Normal pressure for front tires is 21 pounds; for rear, 27 pounds, cool.

(7) *ITEM 46, LEAKS, GENERAL.* Look in engine compartment, under vehicle and fuel tank, for indications of fuel or oil leaks. Trace all leaks to their source, and correct or report any leaks found.

(8) *ITEM 51, BODY AND TOP.* Inspect

body, doors, windshield, top, and seats for good condition.

(9) *ITEM 47, ACCESSORIES AND BELTS.* Inspect all accessories for loose mountings and incorrect alignment. Generator and blower belt must not be frayed or broken, and should have $7/16$- to $5/8$-inch deflection (finger pressure).

(10) *ITEM 48, AIR CLEANER.* If vehicle has been operated under extremely dusty or sandy conditions, examine element for excessive dirt and oil level. Service as necessary.

(11) *ITEM 49, FENDERS.* Inspect fenders for loose mountings and damaged condition.

TOP The front axle. The ends of the torque rod housings can be seen, each holding four steel bands. *(Author's collection)*

ABOVE Another view showing the connection between the front axle and wheel; we can see the two support arms linking out from the torque rods. *(Author's collection)*

RIGHT A Type 166 headlight, with canvas low-visibility cover. *(Author's collection)*

RIGHT A standard German Army blowtorch, an essential piece of cold weather kit for Kübelwagen and Schwimmwagen maintenance. *(Author's collection)*

(12) ITEM 50, TOWING CONNECTIONS. Towing hooks must be in good condition with latches working properly.
(13) ITEM 52, GLASS. Clean windshield, rear vision mirrors, and light lenses. Inspect for looseness and damage.
(War Department, 1944, pp. 28–29)

In the German forces, any modifications or repairs to vehicles would be diligently recorded in the vehicle's *Begleitheft* (Technical Log Book), so that future mechanics could identify the vehicle's previous problems.

Environmental problems

Much of the mechanical effort expended in keeping the Kübelwagen and Schwimmwagen operable was the result of damage sustained in the field. Battlefields and operational theatres have always been hard on vehicles. In extreme situations, vehicles are pushed to and beyond their own limits, typically driven longer, harder and further than in peacetime conditions and through weathers that might, in happier times, keep them locked in garages.

There are some extremely useful reports produced following wartime Kübelwagen test drives, in which vehicles were put through arduous in-theatre slogs and the mechanical issues recorded in reports for the benefit of manufacturers and users. One of the most

RIGHT A Schwimmwagen rolls along a road in France; the sign warns German vehicle crews about the dangers of strafing aircraft. *(Cody Images)*

ABOVE The standard Wehrmacht battery heater. In winter conditions one of these oil heaters would be placed in the battery box to keep the battery warm. *(Author's collection)*

US KÜBELWAGEN MANUAL ADVICE – TOWING THE VEHICLE

a. Towing to Start the Vehicle. This method of starting the engine can be used where the power from the battery is insufficient. Two riveted hooks are provided on the front of the vehicle for cable attachment. Preliminary inspection of the vehicle must take place before any towing action is allowed. The towing vehicle must effect a gradual start to avoid any undue strain and must be driven in first gear during the entire towing operation. High speed is unnecessary. The fuel cock and the ignition switch of the towed vehicle must be turned to the 'ON' position, the clutch pedal must be fully depressed, the gearshift lever placed in the third position, and the choke lever pulled all the way out. Release the parking brake. The signal can now be given to the towing vehicle to start. When normal speed has been reached, release the clutch pedal gradually until the firing action takes place in the engine. Then depress the clutch pedal immediately and push the choke button in part way. Keep the engine going by joint action of the accelerator and choke, until it is warm enough to make the choke action unnecessary.

b. Towing Disabled Vehicle. Two hooks are bolted in place on the rear of the vehicle identical with those on the front, for cable attachment when the vehicle is disabled. Under normal conditions the vehicle can be towed from the front, but where damage is apparent in the transmission or rear axle, the vehicle can be hoisted clear of the ground by the rear hooks, and towed on its front wheels.

(War Department, 1944, p. 13)

enlightening was a mass vehicle test conducted between 2 August and 30 September 1941. The trial involved a round trip of more than 10,000km (6,213 miles) made by 43 vehicles, including a regular KdF-Wagen sedan, two VW Type 87s and two Type 82s. The route of the trip was a circuitous one from the Kummersdorf test centre to Greece, via Czechoslovakia, Hungary, Yugoslavia and Bulgaria, and then back again. It was as much an adventure for the mechanics attending as it was for the vehicles. The landscape was both spectacular and gruelling – the report writer noted that during the journey through Greece, the KdF-Wagen alone made the 25km (15.5-mile) trip through the precipitous Thermopylae Pass no fewer than six times. The summer heat resulted in the vehicles coping with constant intense dust that required the windscreen wipers to be switched on just to maintain visual contact with the vehicle in front.

Although this book is not about the KdF-Wagen per se, the results of its trial are informative. The chief problem, above all others, was the wearing and performance effects caused by the ingress of dust. Almost every part of the vehicle was penetrated by it, including the front luggage compartment, engine compartment and door seals. The motor became regularly choked up with dust, with the distributor, dynamo and oil sump filter especially

BELOW A Type 166 seen at Kursk in 1943. The crew would have to check the vehicle regularly for any build-up of foliage caught in the moving parts. *(Cody Images)*

ABOVE A later
version of the Type
166 Schwimmwagen,
with the side hand
rail running between
the wings and not
extending out from
the body. *(Courtesy
Alain LeGrand)*

RIGHT A view of the
same vehicle from the
other side. Note the
machine gun mounts
fore and aft. *(Courtesy
Alain LeGrand)*

badly affected. The mechanics found that the problem of a dusty dynamo could be solved by sealing the unit with a protective linen shroud. Regarding the oil sump, dust build-up meant that the oil needed changing every 1,000–1,500km (621–932 miles), and after 3,000km (1,864 miles) the system would be completely choked. It was recommended that a felt filter was fitted to strain out the worst of the dust before the air even went into the oil sump filter; this measure was indeed put into action, especially in the North African theatre. Regarding the general oil levels of the vehicle, there was actually little oil loss for most of the journey, apart from some problems with oil-cooler seals during the last third of the journey. Other problems included defective plug leads, a snapped fan belt and bent wheel rims, but on the whole the car ran admirably. It was noted that the brakes and suspension performed extremely well under the conditions, although the reviewer did recommend that the powerplant be upgraded to give more force up gradients and when the car was inevitably overloaded.

Like their sedan siblings, the Type 87s also struggled to cope with the constant inflow of dust and sand. The same parts of the engine were affected, and as with the KdF-Wagen the fitment of a felt air filter dramatically increased the intervals between filter oil changes. The mechanics also installed intake air ducting, which significantly reduced the volume of sand drawn into the engine, although problems with poor rubber seals between the engine compartment and the vehicle body rather negated the benefit.

The problems that afflicted the vehicles eventually ran to quite a substantial list. They included:

■ Abrasion wear on the pistons, cylinders and rod bearings.
■ Collapse of the seal between the carburettor and the intake duct.
■ Damage and wear to rear axle components.
■ Broken steering lever on the shaft.

Yet, once again, the overall mechanical integrity of the vehicles remained intact, albeit with some regular mechanical intervention to cope with the effects of poor conditions.

The experience of the Balkans trip, plus

LEFT Schwimmwagen oil filler. The Kubelwagen and Schwimmwagen both held about 2.5–3 litres (0.5–0.7 Imp gallons) of oil. The lubrication points on Wehrmacht vehicles were normally painted red. (Author's collection)

experience garnered through operations in the North African theatre, led to an ever-expanding body of advice for Kübelwagen mechanics operating in tropical environments. The list of potential problems to look for was long, and they suggest that any mechanic looking after a motor pool in North Africa would have been an overtaxed individual. Some of the general issues defined were:

Fuel stoppages – In very hot climates, it was found that steam bubbles could form in the fuel lines. If these bubbles became trapped between the fuel tank and the pump, the engine would cut out instantly.

BELOW A supply train rolls east with a Kübelwagen onboard. The journey could take many days and the vehicle would require an extensive maintenance check at its destination. (Cody Images)

Fuel evaporation – Tropical temperatures would also cause fuel to evaporate, both from vehicle tanks and from storage canisters. This would affect the distances the Kübelwagen could travel on a tank of fuel, and mechanics also had to keep their fuel stocks as cool as possible.

Rust – Surprisingly, despite the dryness of the desert, rust could still be a problem on vehicles. The dust and stones of the environment would chip away paintwork down to bare metal, and overnight condensation could then cause those parts to rust. For this reason, it was recommended that damaged paintwork be repaired frequently, the maintenance taking place during the cooler evening hours.

Lubrication – Hot temperatures thinned lubricating oil, exacerbating oil loss if there was a leak anywhere on the vehicle. Furthermore, the mechanic had to check that moving parts were not being excessively abraded by oil mixing with dust and, in effect, forming a highly efficient grinding paste.

Condensation – The condensation formed in the cooler evening, night and morning hours could be especially invasive, and cause

problems of its own, especially with the ignition system. The condensation could build up in the distributor, circuit breaker or around the spark plugs, making the vehicle resistant to starting up, especially in the early morning. Proper oiling and air drying helped cope with these problems.

Dust wear – Dust abrasion was found to be particularly acute in the gearbox and axle drive, with wear inflicted upon gear cogs and bearings.

Insects – The desert insect life also had an impact upon the general well-being of the vehicle. Any wooden parts (thankfully on the Kübelwagen they were few) were prey to termites, and leather or textile materials were damaged by other gnawing types of creature.

Like the Germans, the Americans also explored the issues surrounding the use of the Kübelwagen in desert regions, via their small fleet of captured vehicles. The Kübelwagen manual they produced contained an entire section dedicated to maintaining the vehicle in arid and dusty conditions, placing a distinct emphasis on dust control and battery maintenance:

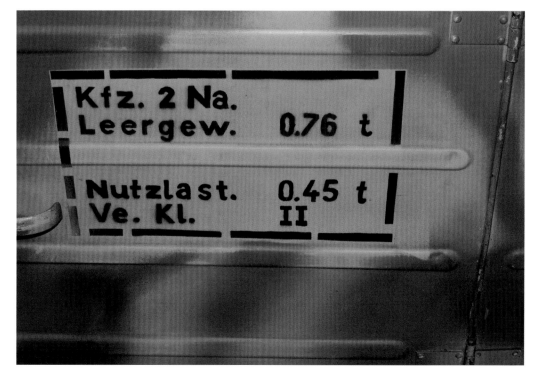

RIGHT The panel on the vehicle door gives information that includes empty weight in metric tonnes (*Leergewicht*), the payload (*Nutzlast*) and the loading class for railway shipping (*Verlade Klasse*). *(Cody Images)*

14. DUSTY CONDITIONS AND HOT WEATHER.

a. Dusty Conditions. When operating under dusty conditions, trouble caused by sand-laden air may be expected unless extra precautions are taken. Clean oil strainer, fuel strainer and sediment bowl frequently. In particularly sandy areas it may be necessary to service the air cleaner every 4 hours or oftener. When filling gasoline and oil tanks, use cloth over filler openings to prevent dirt and dust from entering.

b. Hot Weather.

(1) GENERAL. Since the engine in the Volkswagen is air cooled, high temperatures in the vicinity of operation will be reflected in an increased engine temperature. Keep a close check on the oil level and the viscosity of the lubricant. Examine the fan belt to be sure it is operating the fan at normal speed. See that the cylinder baffles are in place, and that the fan housing is properly connected to provide adequate air circulation around the cylinders.

(2) BATTERY CARE.

(a) Water Level. In torrid zones, check cell water level daily, and replenish, if necessary, with pure distilled water. If this is not available, any water fit to drink may be used. However, continuous use of water with high mineral content will eventually cause damage to the battery and should be avoided.

(b) Specific Gravity. Batteries operating in torrid climates should have a weaker electrolyte than for temperate climates. Instead of 1.300 gravity, the electrolyte should be adjusted to around 1.210 to 1.230 for a fully charged battery. This will prolong the life of the negative plates and separators. Under this condition, a battery should be recharged at about 1.160. Where freezing conditions do not prevail, there is no danger with hydrometer readings from 1.230 to 1.075.

(c) Self-discharge. A battery will self-discharge at a greater rate at high temperatures if standing for long periods. This must be taken into consideration when operating in torrid zones. If necessary to park for several days, remove the battery and store in a cool place.

(War Department, 1944, pp. 17–18)

BELOW An exploded view of the Schwimmwagen's pedal controls and linkages, from the official spare parts manual. *(Wehrmacht, D662/14)*

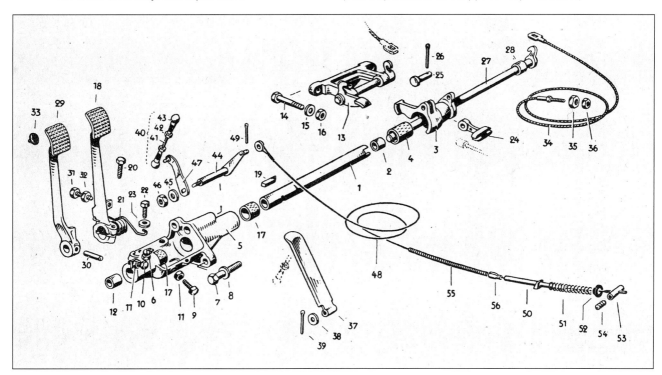

ABOVE The
Schwimmwagen
dashboard. Note
how the single long
fuse box differs from
the two dashboard-
mounted fuse boxes
on the Kübelwagen.
*(Courtesy Oliver
Barnham)*

Cold-climate maintenance

In Chapter 5, we saw how the driver of the Kübelwagen and Schwimmwagen had to negotiate winter conditions, especially in relation to starting procedures and general vehicle care. For mechanics tasked with performing more substantial engineering work, winter conditions were a practical nightmare. The additional strain was only partly due to the diverse range of malfunctions and breakages resulting from driving through landscapes of ice and snow. There was also the factor that performing complex mechanical tasks, especially outdoors, carried extra human issues such as the dangers of frostbite and exposure, the need to wear

RIGHT Under the
Schwimmwagen
dashboard. To the left
of the steering column
is the hand-operated
auxiliary fuel pump. To
the right are two fuel
filters and the fuel tank
on/off switch.

thick gloves when attempting to carry out work requiring manual dexterity, plus the weakening effect of extreme cold upon both tools and component parts. In general, mechanical tasks in the Russian winter would take about two or three times longer than they would on a summer's day in France or Italy.

This was unfortunate, for as robust as the Kübelwagen and Schwimmwagen undoubtedly were, they were mechanically battered by winter conditions on the Eastern Front. Even the simplest component or function had extra issues. Take fluids, for instance. The Kübelwagen and Schwimmwagen benefited greatly on the Eastern Front by being air-cooled, but in sub-zero conditions water could condense out in fuel tanks, causing ice crystals that could block up fuel lines and carburettor jets. When filling the Kübelwagen fuel tank, therefore, the fuel was best poured through a filter of some type, to strain out the ice particles. Also, it was advised to keep the Kübelwagen's tank as full as possible during halts; the more full the tank, the less air space there was for water to condense out into the air.

Lubrication and oiling procedures were critical in sub-zero temperatures. We noted in Chapter 5 how oils had to be thinned with petrol to make them suitable for sub-zero use. If this was not possible, however, it might be the case that the crankcase oil was drained off and kept warm externally to the vehicle.

Electricals also required some special attention (we have already discussed the effects on batteries). With the generator and cranking motor, for example:

Check the brushes, commutators, and bearings. See that the commutators are clean. The large surges of current which occur when starting a cold engine require good contact between brushes and commutators. Be sure that no heavy grease or dirt has been left on the cranking motor throw out mechanism. Heavy grease or dirt may keep the gears from being meshed or cause them to remain in mesh after the engine starts running thus ruining the cranking motor.

(War Department, 1944, p. 16)

RIGHT A grainy German manual photograph shows a mechanic fitting rail wheels to the Kübelwagen, converting the vehicle into a crude locomotive. *(Author's collection)*

Ice and moisture could interfere with lights, spark plugs and wiring, and needed brushing off carefully before the vehicle was operated. The freezing conditions could have an impact on some of the vehicle's major physical components. Given that the shock resistance of metals reduces considerably in freezing conditions, the axles and shock absorbers were particularly vulnerable to impact damage on the ice-hardened ground.

Major component maintenance

A chapter on the mechanical maintenance of the Kübelwagen and Schwimmwagen would be incomplete without some guidance on how to perform some of the key engineering tasks. To accomplish this, at least partially, the remainder of this section contains instructions from the Wehrmacht Operator's Handbook and the US War Department Manual, for the following major tasks: 1) Removing and installing the gearbox and differential, and 2) Removing and installing the engine. Furthermore, the appendix contains a useful troubleshooting guide from the manual, giving reference on how to remedy common problems and issues that mechanics and operators might encounter in the field. With any bare descriptions such as these, it is always worth reminding ourselves that wartime engineers might have to perform such operations with dark enemy clouds on the horizon, in workshops with poor ventilation, low light and inadequate tools. Remarkable men worked on these remarkable vehicles.

LEFT The rail conversion of the Type 82. The driver still maintained limited directional control over the wheels. *(Author's collection)*

RIGHT The Type 166 propeller had a protective housing to shield it from impacts. Note that the propeller could only deliver forward movement, not reverse. *(Courtesy Oliver Barnham)*

a) Removal of the Complete Propeller Assembly

Work Sequence:

1. Undo the nut in the engine compartment which holds the spring to the propeller tensioning wheel.
2. Remove the circlip and the inspection cap on the end of the propeller swivel-mounting shaft. When reassembling, apply sealing compound to the cap.
3. Remove the inner circlip on the swivel-mounting shaft.
4. Remove the two pins that hold the swivel-mounting shaft in place and drive the shaft from the casing (and from the gear wheel to which the tensioning chain is attached).

Attention! Take care not to damage the assembly!

b) Disassembly of the Propeller

Work Sequence:

1. Drain the oil.
2. Remove the splash-plate and the ring-guard, by undoing the 6 bolts on top and the 4 lower bolts that hold the skeg to the drive-chain housing.
3. Remove the propeller fastening cone and pull off the propeller.
4. Remove the circlip which holds the upper drive-shaft in place. To gain access to the clip, unscrew the inspection plug on the drive-chain housing.
5. Take off the housing cover-plate, and remove the drive assembly. Do not dismantle the drive-chain.

c) Propeller Tension Adjustment

When the propeller swivels on its mounting, this movement is transmitted via a chain to a gearwheel in the engine compartment. To this gearwheel is attached a spring which exerts its greatest force when the propeller is up or down. An adjustment nut is provided on the tensioning spring. This adjuster must be set so that the propeller assembly is capable of being raised or lowered and held firmly in either position.

(Wehrmacht, 1942, p. 72)

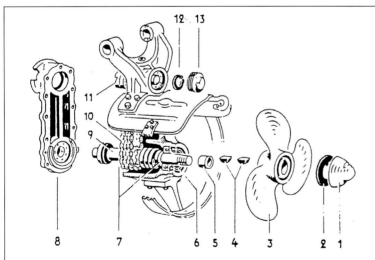

1   Drain the oil.
2   Remove the cone (1) and retaining washer (2) from the end of the propeller shaft.
3   Remove the propeller (3).
4   Remove **both** of the woodruff keys (4).
5   Unscrew the plug (13). When reassembling, apply 'Curil' sealant, and use a punch to secure the plug.
6   Remove the spring-clip (12).
7   Take off the back cover (8). When reassembling, spread the mating surface with 'Curil' sealant.
8   Remove the propeller shaft (9) the vehicle coupling-shaft (11) and the drive chain (10) **all together**. Renew the oil seal (6).

Gearbox and differential

a. Removal. The transmission and differential are removed as a unit. The engine must be removed. ... [Then] Remove the two rear wheels. Remove the two rear brake control cables and the clutch cable. The drive shaft housing assembly must be removed from the rear torque arm; a split bracket on the drive shaft housing fits into a groove on the rear torque arm and is secured by three bolts, lock washers, and hex nuts. The inboard section of this split bracket is held tight to the drive shaft housing by two bolts, lock washers, and hex nuts, and these hex nuts must be backed off to

LEFT Removal and installation of parts in the propeller housing. Replacing the driving chain. VW Type 7 (166). *(Courtesy Oliver Barnham)*

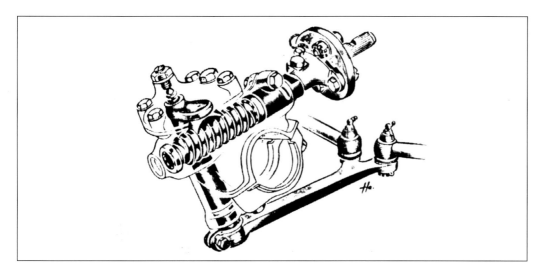

allow this bracket to slide inward, relieving the tension on the rear torque arm in order that it may be withdrawn from the bracket. Remove the rear shock absorbers. The transmission shift rod must be disconnected from the gearshift rod at the universal joint at the top rear of the tunnel inside the vehicle. Remove the rear set screw with a socket head wrench. The differential and transmission support arms fasten to the bell housing support and are secured by two cap screws; these two cap screws must be removed. Remove two bolts, hex nuts, and lock washers from the front power train mount, withdraw the transmission and differential housing to the rear until the transmission shift rod is clear of the front power train mount, and then lower.

b. Installation. Raise the transmission and differential housing into position between the support arms, and insert the transmission shift rod into the front power train mount and align properly with the gearshift rod at the universal joint on top the tunnel, inside and at the rear of the vehicle. Secure the transmission and differential housing to the support arms with two cap screws. Secure the housing at the front power train mount with two bolts, lock washers, and nuts. Install a set screw into the universal joint, securing the transmission shift rod to the

gearshift rod. Fit the split bracket on the end
of the drive shaft housing to the torque rod
arm and install three bolts, lock washers, and
hex nuts. Tighten the inboard section of this
split bracket at the clamp connection, which
prevents it sliding on the drive shaft housing.
These last two steps must be carried out on
both sides of the vehicle at the torque rod arms.
Install the two rear wheels. Install the two rear
brake control cables and the clutch cable.

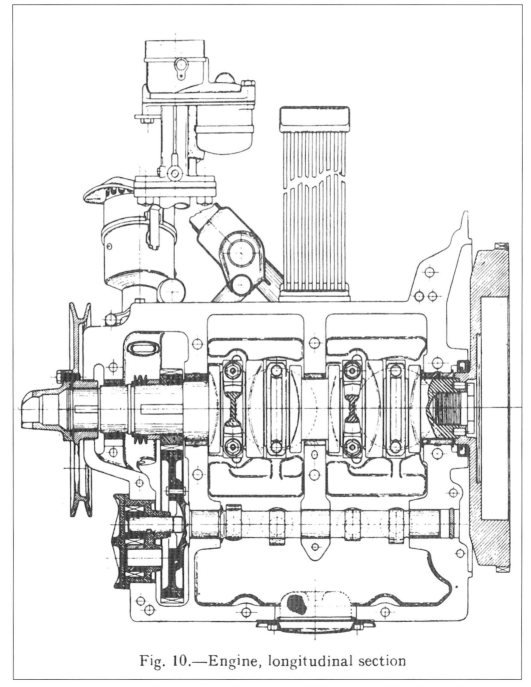

Fig. 10.—Engine, longitudinal section

Engine removal

a. General. The Volkswagen engine is removed by lowering it to a dolly or other type of support.

b. Disconnect battery cable from cranking motor.

c. Shut off the fuel supply by turning the fuel cock under the fuel tank in a clockwise direction. Disconnect the gasoline pipe (tank to fuel pump) at the fuel pump.

d. Remove the oil-bath air cleaner by loosening the C-clamp connection at the carburetor and by withdrawing the air intake rubber hose from the port hole in the left wall of the engine compartment.

e. Disconnect the choke and throttle cables at the carburetor.

f. Remove generator. Remove the retainer nut which holds the generator drive pulley to generator, and remove the pulley and belt.

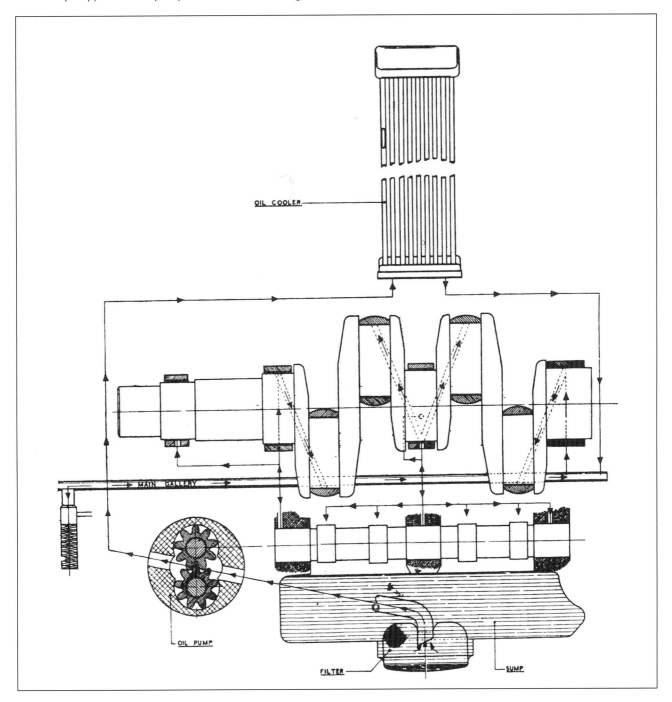

h. Disconnect low and high tension wires at distributor.

i. Remove four bolts which hold the front protection pan to the floor and remove the pan.

j. Remove two bolts which hold cranking motor to housing, and remove cranking motor.

k. Remove engine. Two bolts and two studs hold the engine cylinder block to the flywheel housing. The upper right bolt was removed when the cranking motor was removed. Remove the upper left bolt, and remove nuts from the two lower studs. Pull the engine toward the rear of the vehicle until it is free of the clutch shaft, and lower it to the floor. Be careful to support the engine as it is being moved toward the rear of the vehicle so its weight will not be supported by the clutch shaft.

Engine installation

a. Raise the engine in position, supporting the weight as the clutch shaft is entered through the clutch disk hub. Install the upper left bolt to flywheel housing, and install two stud nuts.

b. Install cranking motor to flywheel housing by installing two retaining bolts.

c. Install front protection pan by installing four retaining bolts.

d. Connect high and low tension wires to distributor.

e. Place front cowling in position and install metal screw at each end.

f. Install generator. Work the left end of the fan housing in position over the oil cooler and lower the generator to its mounting bracket. Install and tighten the C-clamp. Connect generator regulator wires. Place the fan belt on the generator drive pulley and place the pulley on the generator shaft. Install nut which holds pulley to shaft.

g. Insert the air cleaner intake hose to the pipe in the left side of the engine compartment, and connect the air cleaner to the carburettor.

h. Connect gasoline line to fuel pump, and open fuel tank shut-off cock.

i. Connect cable to cranking motor.

j. Connect choke and throttle controls to carburetor.

ABOVE The Schwimmwagen engine, with a good view of the cold-weather starter fuel tank at the top right, with the fuel tap on top of the fuel pump. Note the two fan belts under the belt cover; the Kübelwagen had just one belt. *(Courtesy Oliver Barnham)*

Disconnect the two wires at the regulator. Loosen the C-clamp connection in front of the generator regulator and slide the clamp toward the fan housing. Remove the screw at each end of the fan housing which fastens the housing to the engine. In lifting this assembly clear, tilt the left side upward to avoid the oil cooler mounted within the fan housing.

g. Remove cowling at the front of the engine compartment by removing the metal screw at each end which secures the cowling at the base of the compartment.

In many ways, the Kübelwagen and Schwimmwagen were unremarkable vehicles. They did not have a significant effect on the course or outcome of the war. They were not produced in large numbers, certainly not when compared to many other vehicle types. They did not have the offensive firepower of an armoured car, nor the carrying capacity of a truck.

Yet what these two vehicles achieved, and the reason why the Allies and posterity took such an interest in them, is what they embody. The Kübelwagen and Schwimmwagen illustrate a near-perfect marriage between vehicle, user and tactical requirements. The apparent simplicity of both vehicles is the result of a substantial investment in engineering that produced enduring mechanical innovations. Sometimes vehicles excel simply because they do their job perfectly, without fuss or strain. Arguably, this is what has made the Kübelwagen and Schwimmwagen so remarkable.

ABOVE A Kübelwagen run by the Feldgendarmerie. Some form of extra cover is provided over the spare wheel mount, and the operator has improvised spare fuel tank mounts to the front body. *(BArch)*

BELOW A Kübelwagen is carried inside a Junkers Ju52 aircraft for shipping to Crete or North Africa. *(Cody Images)*

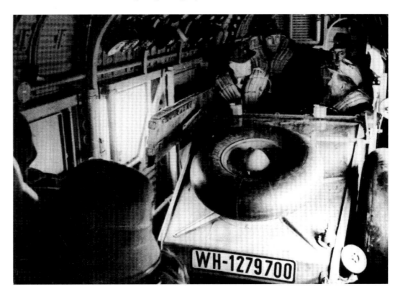

Appendix

Kübelwagen/Schwimmwagen Troubleshooting Guide

26. GENERAL.

a. This section contains troubleshooting information and tests which can be made to help determine the causes of some of the troubles that may develop in the Volkswagen used under average climatic conditions (above 32°F). Each symptom of trouble given under the individual unit or system is followed by a list of possible causes of the trouble. The tests necessary to determine which one of the possible causes is responsible for the trouble are explained after each possible cause.

27. ENGINE.

a. Engine Will Not Turn.

  (1) HYDROSTATIC LOCK OR SEIZURE. Remove spark plugs and attempt to turn engine with hand crank to check for excess fuel or oil in cylinders. If engine turns, the lock will be relieved. If engine will not turn, test for jammed cranking motor throwout mechanism (step (2), following).

  (2) CRANKING. MOTOR THROWOUT MECHANISM JAMMED. Remove cranking motor. Clean grease and dirt from throwout mechanism. Inspect mechanism for broken parts, repair, and install cranking motor. If engine still will not turn, notify higher authority.

  (3) INCORRECT OIL VISCOSITY. Drain crankcase and refill with proper grade oil.

b. Engine Turns But Will Not Start.

  (1) INOPERATIVE FUEL SYSTEM. Remove fuel line from carburetor. With ignition switch off, turn engine over with the cranking motor. If fuel does not flow freely, it is not reaching carburetor. If fuel flows freely, trouble is in carburetor. Repair or replace faulty carburetor.

  (2) INOPERATIVE IGNITION SYSTEM. Remove a cable from a spark plug. Turn ignition switch to 'ON' Hold spark plug cable terminal ¼ inch from engine casting, and crank engine. If spark does not jump the ¼-inch gap, the ignition is inadequate.

c. Engine Does Not Develop Full Power.

  (1) IMPROPER IGNITION (par. 32).

  (2) IMPROPER VALVE ADJUSTMENT. Check clearance, and adjust if necessary.

  (3) USE OF IMPROPER TYPE OF FUEL. Change to fuel of correct specifications.

  (4) PREIGNITION. If proper octane fuel is being used and the ignition system is functioning satisfactorily, spark plug of improper heat range may be the cause of the trouble. Otherwise notify higher authority.

  (5) AIR LEAKS AT CARBURETOR OR MANIFOLD FLANGES. With engine running at 800 revolutions per minute, apply a small amount of oil at carburetor and manifold flange gaskets. If oil is sucked in, there is a leak. If leak persists after tightening flange bolt nuts, replace gaskets.

  (6) LOW ENGINE COMPRESSION OR IMPROPER VALVE TIMING. If the engine does not develop full power with fuel reaching combustion chambers, adequate ignition, and the proper grade and quantity of oil in crankcase, low compression or improper valve timing is indicated. Notify higher authority.

d. Engine Misfires.

  (1) FAULTY IGNITION SYSTEM (par. 32).

  (2) LOW ENGINE COMPRESSION (step c (6) above).

  (3) INCORRECT CARBURETOR ADJUSTMENT. Adjust carburetor (par. 64 b).

  (4) CLOGGED FUEL TANK CAP VENT. Open vents or replace cap.

  (5) RESTRICTED FUEL FLOW (par. 29 a (2) and b).

  (6) WATER IN FUEL. Remove sediment bowl from bottom of fuel tank and inspect for water. If found, drain all fuel from system and refill with pure gasoline.

e. Excessive Oil Consumption.

  (1) OIL VISCOSITY TOO LOW. Drain crankcase, and refill with proper oil.

  (2) EXTERNAL OIL LEAKS. Inspect for oil leaks at oil connections and gaskets, and tighten loose connections. If leakage is detected at main bearing flanges, notify higher authority.

  (3) PISTON AND RINGS WORN OR DAMAGED. Notify higher authority.

f. Engine Will Not Stop.

  (1) DEFECTIVE IGNITION SWITCH. Replace switch (par. 115).

  (2) ENGINE OVERHEATED. Check oil temperature gage for evidence of high oil temperature. Determine if all cooling surfaces are free from dirt and oil.

28. CLUTCH.

a. Clutch Slips.

  (1) CLUTCH PEDAL OR LINKAGE BENT OR BINDING. Disconnect linkage and inspect for bent or binding part. Replace defective parts (par. 52 c).

  (2) CLUTCH WORN OR BROKEN INTERNALLY. If linkage is in satisfactory condition and slippage cannot be removed through adjustment, internal wear or breakage is indicated. Notify higher authority.

b. Clutch Grabs.

  (1) LOOSE MOUNTING. Tighten external mounting nuts.

  (2) INTERNAL DIFFICULTY. If tightening external mounting nuts fails to remove trouble, internal difficulty is indicated. Notify higher authority.

c. Clutch Rattles.

  (1) LOOSE OR WORN CONTROL LINKAGE. Inspect clutch linkage. Replace worn parts and tighten loose parts.

  (2) INTERNAL DIFFICULTY. If rattle persists with linkage in satisfactory condition, notify higher authority.

d. Clutch Will Not Release.

  (1) CLUTCH LINKAGE OUT OF ADJUSTMENT. Adjust clutch linkage (par. 56 c). Replace defective parts of linkage.

  (2) INTERNAL DIFFICULTY. If clutch cannot be adjusted to release, and linkage is in satisfactory condition and adjustment, notify higher authority.

e. Clutch Makes a Scrubbing Noise.

  (1) CLUTCH SLEEVE SCORED OR RIDGED. Notify higher authority.

29. FUEL SYSTEM.

a. Fuel Does Not Reach Carburetor.

  (1) CLOGGED FUEL TANK VENT. Remove obstruction from vent or replace cap.

  (2) INOPERATIVE FUEL PUMP, CLOGGED FUEL FILTER OR LINES. Remove sediment bowl from bottom of fuel tank and check passage from tank by blowing through line. If obstruction is indicated remove and clean fuel line. Service fuel filter, and if passage to fuel pump is unobstructed, reconnect fuel line. Disconnect fuel line to carburetor from fuel pump. Turn engine over by means of cranking motor. If fuel does not flow from pump, a defective pump is indicated. Otherwise, the fuel line from pump to carburetor is obstructed. Replace defective parts (par. 63).

b. Fuel Does Not Reach Cylinders.

  (1) CARBURETOR STRAINER CLOGGED. Clean or replace strainer.

  (2) THROTTLE NOT OPENING. Adjust throttle.

  (3) CARBURETOR JETS CLOGGED. Replace carburetor (par. 64 c and d).

BELOW This Schwimmwagen (seen here in Australia after its restoration by owner Ray Black) was dispatched from VW's Wolfsburg factory in 1944 only a few weeks before the facility was virtually destroyed by Allied bombing. *(Ray Black, Australia)*

30. INTAKE AND EXHAUST SYSTEM.

a. Air Passage to Carburetor Restricted.

    (1) AIR CLEANER DIRTY. Service air cleaner (par. 66).

    (2) AIR INTAKE TUBE CRUSHED. Visually inspect tube. Replace if damaged (par. 66).

b. Dirt Laden Air Entering Carburetor.

    (1) AIR CLEANER DIRTY. Service air cleaner (par. 19).

    (2) NO OIL IN AIR CLEANER. Service air cleaner (par. 19).

    (3) AIR PIPE DISCONNECTED OR LOOSELY CONNECTED. Connect air pipe tightly.

c. Exhaust Makes Excessive Noise and/or System Emits Gas.

    (1) MANIFOLD GASKETS LEAKING. Inspect gaskets with engine running. If gaskets are leaking, tighten manifold attaching nuts. If leak persists, notify higher authority.

    (2) LEAK AT EXHAUST PIPE FLANGE. Visually inspect connection with engine running. If gasket leaks, tighten nuts. If leak persists, replace gasket (par. 49 c).

    (3) EXHAUST PIPE BROKEN OR BENT. Inspect pipe with engine running and replace muffler if broken or bent (par. 49 c).

    (4) MUFFLER DEFECTIVE. If other parts of system are in satisfactory condition and excessive noise persists, replace muffler (par. 49 c).

BELOW Schwimmwagen interior and dashboard. Note jack at far left of dashboard, tool box at far right, and red handle in the centre that operates the central lubrication pump. *(Courtesy Oliver Barnham)*

31. COOLING SYSTEM

a. Engine Overheats.

    (1) FAN BELT LOOSE OR BROKEN. Inspect fan belt. Replace if broken (par. 51), adjust tension if loose.

    (2) CAUSED BY CONDITION EXTERNAL TO COOLING SYSTEM. If the cause for overheating cannot be located within the cooling system, check for ignition, dragging brakes, insufficient lubrication, and incorrect valve timing.

32. IGNITION SYSTEM.

(1) SPARK PLUGS FAULTY. Uneven operation at idle speed, misfiring at high speed, or loss of power, may be due to faulty spark plugs. Remove and inspect spark plugs (par. 75), and replace faulty plugs.

(2) DISTRIBUTOR POINTS FAULTY. Hard starting or complete failure to start on the part of the engine may be due to faulty distributor points. Remove distributor cap and inspect points. Measure gap. Crank engine and observe opening and closing of points. Adjust points if out of adjustment (par. 45 c). Replace distributor if action of opening and closing mechanism is faulty. Refer old distributor to higher authority for repair or rebuilding.

(3) IGNITION COIL OR CONDENSER FAULTY. Weak or no spark, with fully charged battery and serviceable spark plugs and distributor points installed, may indicate a faulty ignition coil or condenser. Remove suspected coil and/or condenser, and replace it with a part known to function properly (pars. 14 and 74 d).

33. STARTING AND GENERATING SYSTEM.

a. Low Generator Output.

   (1) BATTERY FULLY CHARGED. No repair is necessary.

   (2) DIRT ON COMMUTATOR. Remove inspection cover from generator. If dirt can be seen on commutator bars, start engine and hold a piece of 2/0 flintpaper against bars. Blow dust from generator with dry compressed air.

   (3) BRUSHES WORN. Inspect brushes and replace if worn.

   (4) GENERATOR REGULATOR OUT OF ADJUSTMENT. If trouble is not due to one of above causes, replace regulator.

   (5) CAUSES EXTERNAL TO GENERATOR. Low generator output can be caused by high resistance in either battery or in wiring between the generator and batteries. Check all wiring connections to be sure they are clean and tight. Test individual wires with a test lamp. Test dual unit filter, and generator condenser. Clean and tighten all connections. If trouble persists, replace the battery.

b. Unsteady or Insufficient Generator Output.

   (1) DIRT ON COMMUTATOR (step a (2) above).

   (2) BRUSHES WORN (step a (3) above).

   (3) SHORTED, OPEN, OR GROUNDED WIRING: LOOSE, OPEN, OR DIRTY CONNECTION. Inspect all wiring. Use test lamp to test individual wires. Clean and tighten all connections. Replace or repair broken or poorly insulated wires.

   (4) GENERATOR REGULATOR INOPERATIVE. Inspect regulator.

c. High Generator Output.

   (1) LOW BATTERY. Test battery with a hydrometer. If specific gravity is below 1.275, high generator output is normal, and no repair necessary.

   (2) HIGH RESISTANCE WIRING. Inspect wiring, using test lamp on individual wires. Clean and tighten all connections, and replace defective wires.

   (3) OVERHEATED BATTERY. Feel battery case, and if hot to touch allow it to cool. Add water before again using.

   (4) VOLTAGE REGULATOR INOPERATIVE. Test operation of voltage regulator.

   (5) SHORTED OR GROUNDED GENERATOR FIELD CIRCUIT. If none of the above causes are at fault, a shorted or grounded field circuit is indicated. Replace generator, and refer old generator to higher authority.

d. Noisy Generator.

   (1) MOUNTING BOLTS LOOSE. Attempt to tighten mounting bolts.

   (2) LACK OF LUBRICATION. Lubricate generator.

   (3) WORN COMMUTATOR OR BEARINGS. If noise persists after tightening and lubricating, replace generator.

e. Cranking Motor Inoperative.

   (1) DISCHARGED BATTERY. Check battery (par. 34).

   (2) BROKEN BATTERY CABLE OR TERMINAL. Inspect cables from batteries to ground, and from batteries to cranking motor. Replace broken cables.

   (3) INOPERATIVE SWITCH. Short circuit terminals of switch with a heavy metal tool pressed firmly across terminals. If cranking motor operates, an inoperative switch is indicated. Replace switch.

   (4) INTERNAL DEFECT IN CRANKING MOTOR. Disconnect cable from cranking motor, and press on cranking motor switch. Touch end of cable to frame of vehicle for an instant. Sparks indicate that the inoperative cranking motor has internal defect. Replace cranking motor.

34. BATTERY AND LIGHTING SYSTEM.

a. Battery Cells All Test Over 1.250 Specific Gravity and Within 15 Points of Each Other.

   (1) BATTERY NORMAL. No corrective measures are necessary in summer. For cold weather operation, give batteries booster charge if cells are under 1.275.

b. Battery Cells All Test Under 1.250 Specific Gravity and Within 15 Points of Each Other.

   (1) DEMAND FROM BATTERIES EXCEEDS INPUT FROM GENERATOR. Recharge batteries, check electrical system for short circuits, loose connections, and low generator output.

c. Cells of Battery Vary by 15 or More Points from Each Other with Highest Cell Reading 1.225 Specific Gravity or Over.

   (1) SHORT CIRCUIT IN LOW CELL OR CELLS. Make a momentary high rate test on each cell. If cells vary by more than $\frac{1}{10}$ volt from each other, replace battery; otherwise, recharge until gravity of electrolyte remains constant for four hours. Adjust gravity of all cells by adding water or small amounts of sulphuric acid (1.400 specific gravity or less).

   (2) EVAPORATION CAUSED BY OVERCHARGING. Treat battery as in step (1) above.

   (3) UNNECESSARY ADDITION OF ACID. Treat battery as in step (1) above.

   (4) LOSS OF ELECTROLYTE BY LEAKAGE. Replace battery if case is broken, and refer used battery to higher authority. If electrolyte was lost by tipping battery or by missing caps, treat battery as outlined in step (1) above.

d. Cells of Battery Vary by 15 or More Points from Each Other with Highest Cell Reading Under 1.225 Specific Gravity.

(1) SHORT CIRCUIT IN LOW CELL OR CELLS. Recharge battery if possible. Then make a momentary high rate discharge test. If battery fails to recharge or if cells vary by $1/10$ or more volts after recharge, replace battery. Otherwise adjust gravity of all cells by adding water or small amounts of sulphuric acid (1.400 specific gravity or less).

(2) EVAPORATION CAUSED BY OVERCHARGING. Treat battery as outlined in step (1) above.

(3) UNNECESSARY ADDITION OF ACID. Treat battery as given in step (1) above.

(4) LOSS OF ELECTROLYTE BY LEAKAGE. Replace battery if case is broken. If electrolyte was lost by tipping battery, treat as outlined in step (1) above.

e. Cells of Battery Test Over 1.300 Specific Gravity at 80°F.

(1) UNNECESSARY ADDITION OF ACID. Drain all solutions from battery. Refill with dilute (1.100 specific gravity) electrolyte, and charge at low rate until electrolyte remains constant for four hours. Drain cells again, and refill with 1.285 specific gravity electrolyte. Charge for three hours, adjust gravity to 1.285, and continue charging until gravity of all cells is constant for two hours. If this proves impossible, replace battery (par. 80 d).

(2) ADDITION OF BATTERY COMPOUND OF 'DOPE' SOLUTIONS. Try treating battery as outlined in step (1) above, then replace if necessary.

f. Battery Fully Charged but Tests 1.265 Specific Gravity or Less at 80°F.

(1) EXCESSIVE EVAPORATION USUALLY CAUSED BY OVERCHARGING. Add small amounts of acid (1.400 specific gravity or less) to cells to adjust electrolyte to 1.285 specific gravity.

g. Frequent Additions of Water Necessary.

(1) BROKEN BATTERY CASE. Replace battery, and refer used battery to higher authority.

h. Bulge in Battery Case.

(1) EXCESSIVE TEMPERATURE DUE TO OVERCHARGING. Treat battery as outlined in step d (1) above.

i. Corrosion on Battery Terminals.

(1) EXCESSIVE CHARGING RATE CAUSING ACID TO SPRAY ON TERMINALS. Remove terminals from posts. Clean posts and terminals thoroughly, and replace cable if terminal is weakened by corrosion. Connect terminals and apply a film of No. 2 general purpose grease or vaseline to exposed metal.

(2) LEAD COATING ON TERMINALS DESTROYED. Proceed as directed in step (1) above.

j. Broken Terminal Post on Battery.

(1) LOOSE BATTERY INSTALLATION. Replace battery (par. 82 d).

(2) BATTERY CABLE TOO SHORT. Replace battery and cable (par. 82 d).

k. All Lamps Fail to Light.

(1) CIRCUIT BREAKER OPEN. Close circuit breaker. If it snaps open again, look for short circuit.

(2) BATTERIES DEAD. Check for cause, including short circuits, and eliminate. Recharge, or replace, batteries.

(3) OPEN CIRCUIT IN CABLES OR WIRES. Inspect wiring, and if open circuit cannot be seen, locate with test lamp. Connect disconnected wires or cables and replace broken wires or cables.

l. One Lamps Fails to Light.

(1) BURNED OUT BULB. Replace bulb.

(2) BULB LOOSE IN SOCKET. Install bulb properly.

(3) OPEN CIRCUIT IN CIRCUIT TO LAMP. Proceed as directed in step k (3) above.

(4) LIGHT NOT GROUNDED. Remove light, and clean points of contact on light and vehicle until shiny. Install light.

35. TRANSMISSION.

a. Transmission Noisy.

(1) INCORRECT OR INSUFFICIENT LUBRICANT. Check lubricant and lubricate if necessary.

(2) TRANSMISSION CASE LOOSE ON CLUTCH HOUSING. Tighten housing.

(3) INTERNAL DEFECT. If noise persists after above measures have been taken, report trouble to higher authority.

b. Gears Slip Out of Mesh.

(1) INTERNAL DEFECT. Report condition to higher authority.

c. Lubricant Leaks from Case.

(1) LOOSE CASE BOLTS. Tighten case.

(2) INTERNAL DEFECT. Report condition to higher authority.

36. FRONT AXLE.

a. Hub Overheated.

(1) LACK OF LUBRICATION. Lubricate properly (par. 19 d (5)).

(2) WHEEL BEARINGS TOO TIGHT. Adjust wheel bearings.

b. Rumbling Noise Noticeable Only When Coasting.

(1) WHEEL BEARINGS WORN. Replace wheel bearings.

37. REAR AXLE.

a. Continuous Rumbling Noise.

    (1) LACK OF, OR IMPROPER, LUBRICATION. Lubricate properly (par. 19 d (5)).

    (2) BEARINGS TOO TIGHT. Adjust wheel bearings.

b. Rumbling Noise Noticeable Only When Coasting.

    (1) WORN BEARINGS. Replace wheel bearings.

38. SERVICE BRAKE SYSTEM.

a. Brake Pedal Goes to Floor Board.

    (1) NORMAL WEAR OF BRAKE LINING. Adjust brakes. If worn so that adjustment fails to eliminate trouble, notify higher authority.

b. Brakes Drag.

    (1) BRAKE CONTROL ROD ADJUSTED TOO SHORT. Remove clevis pin and loosen lock nut. Turn yoke counterclockwise to lengthen rod. Tighten lock nut and connect rod.

    (2) BRAKE CONTROL ROD RETURN SPRING WEAKENED OR BROKEN. Remove spring from control rod. Replace with serviceable spring.

c. One Brake Drags.

    (1) GREASE ON BRAKE LINING. Replace brake shoes (pars. 101, 102, and 103). Return old shoes to third echelon for relining. Check condition of grease retainers, and replace if defective.

    (2) BRAKE SHOES OUT OF ADJUSTMENT. Adjust brakes (par. 103).

    (3) LINING LOOSENED FROM SHOE. Replace brake shoe (par. 103).

    (4) BRAKE SHOE SPRING WEAKENED OR BROKEN. Replace brake shoe spring (par. 103).

    (5) BRAKE ANCHOR PIN TIGHT. Replace brake anchor pin (par. 103).

    (6) WHEEL BEARINGS OUT OF ADJUSTMENT. Adjust wheel bearings.

d. Vehicle Pulls to Right or Left When Brakes are Applied and/or Brakes are Uneven.

    (1) BRAKE ON FRONT WHEEL DRAGGING (step c above).

    (2) BRAKES NEED ADJUSTING OR LUBRICATING. Adjust (par. 103 b) and/or lubricate brakes.

    (3) BRAKES NEED RELINING. Report to higher authority.

    (4) GREASE ON BRAKE LINING (step c (1) above).

    (5) BRAKE SHOE RELEASE SPRING BROKEN. Replace broken spring.

    (6) BRAKE DRUM OUT OF ROUND. Replace drum, and return used parts to higher authority.

e. Brakes Take Hold Slowly.

    (1) BRAKES OUT OF ADJUSTMENT. Adjust brakes (par. 103).

    (2) BRAKE LINING WORN. Replace brake shoes (par. 103).

    (3) BRAKE DRUMS WORN. Replace hubs. Return used parts to higher authority.

    (4) BRAKE MECHANISM NEEDS LUBRICATION. Lubricate vehicle.

f. Brakes Release Slowly.

    (1) BRAKE CONTROL ROD NOT RETURNING PROPERLY. Check adjustment of control rod and adjust if necessary. Check condition of brake control rod return spring, and replace spring if broken or weakened.

    (2) BRAKE SHOE OPERATING LEVER BINDING. Lubricate brake shoe operating lever with engine oil. CAUTION: Do not get oil on lining.

    (3) BRAKES NEED ADJUSTING OR LUBRICATING. Adjust (par. 103) and/or lubricate brakes.

g. Insufficient Brakes.

    (1) BRAKES NEED ADJUSTING, LUBRICATING, OR RELINING. Adjust (par. 103), lubricate (par. 19) brakes, or report to higher authority.

h. Brakes Do Not Release.

    (1) BRAKE RIGGING BINDING. Straighten or replace bent parts, and replace worn or broken parts. Lubricate rigging.

i. Brakes Grab.

    (1) GREASE ON LINING. Report to higher authority.

    (2) BRAKE DRUM OUT OF ROUND. Replace drum (par. 100 c).

    (3) BRAKE RIGGING BINDING. Straighten or replace bent parts, and replace broken and worn parts. Lubricate rigging.

BELOW The hull of a Schwimmwagen belonging to the Das Reich Division, still hanging in a Normandy barn in 2015 – wounds untreated. *(Courtesy Alain LeGrand)*

39. PARKING BRAKE SYSTEM.

a. Brake Does Not Hold.
  (1) BRAKE OUT OF ADJUSTMENT. Adjust brake (par. 101).
  (2) BRAKE LINING WORN. Try adjusting brakes (par. 101); if trouble persists, replace shoes (par. 100 d).
  (3) BRAKE SHOE LINING GLAZED OR GREASED. Replace brake shoes (par. 103).

40. WHEELS, HUBS, WHEEL BEARINGS, AND TIRES.

a. Pounding or Squeaking Noise in Wheel.
  (1) WHEEL HUB STUD CAP NUTS LOOSE. Tighten cap nuts.
  (2) TIRE MOUNTED OUT OF BALANCE. Disassemble tire, and assemble correctly (pars. 109 and 110).

b. Wheel Drags and Wheel Bearing Heats.
  (1) WHEEL BEARING ADJUSTED TOO TIGHT. Adjust wheel bearing.

c. Tires Overheat.
  (1) TIRES UNDERINFLATED. Inflate tires to correct pressure (par. 108 a)

d. Excessive or Uneven Tire Wear.
  (1) TIRES INFLATED INCORRECTLY. Inflate tires to correct pressure (par. 108 a).
  (2) TOE-IN OUT OF ADJUSTMENT. Adjust toe-in (par. 110).
  (3) TIRES MOUNTED OUT OF BALANCE. Remove tires and mount correctly (par. 110).

41. SHOCK ABSORBERS.

a. Vehicle Buttons or Skews.
  (1) SHOCK ABSORBER INOPERATIVE. Replace shock absorber (pars. 111, 112, and 113).

b. Exaggerated Spring Action.
  (1) SHOCK ABSORBER INOPERATIVE. Replace shock absorber.

42. STEERING GEAR.

a. Front Wheels Shimmy.
  (1) WHEEL AND TIRE OUT OF BALANCE. Inspect tire. If incorrectly mounted, dismount tire and assemble correctly. If this does not remedy the trouble, refer the wheel and tire to higher authority for balancing.
  (2) STEERING GEAR OUT OF ADJUSTMENT. Adjust steering gear (par. 106 b).
  (3) STEERING GEAR WORN. Refer to higher authority.
  (4) FRONT WHEEL BENT. Jack up front of vehicle, spin wheels, and look for wobble. Replace bent wheel.
  (5) LOOSE FRONT WHEEL BEARINGS. Jack up vehicle, and check bearings for play. Adjust loose bearing.

  (6) FRONT TIRE, WHEEL AND/OR HUB OUT OF BALANCE. Jack up front of vehicle, spin wheels repeatedly, and notice if they always stop and rock at same point. If out of balance, check mounting of tire. If trouble persists, refer entire assembly to higher authority for balancing.
  (7) IMPROPER CASTER OR CAMBER. Notify higher authority.

b. Front Wheel Wanders.
  (1) WORN STEERING GEAR. Replace steering gear. Refer to higher authority.

c. Vehicle Steers With Difficulty.
  (1) STEERING GEAR AND/OR FRONT AXLE LACK PROPER LUBRICATION. Lubricate vehicle correctly (par. 19).
  (2) TIRES UNDERINFLATED. Inflate tires correctly (par. 108 a).
  (3) WORN STEERING GEAR. Replace steering gear (par. 103 b, c and d), and refer used steering gear to higher authority.

d. Road Shocks Felt at Steering Wheel.
  (1) WORN STEERING GEAR. Replace steering gear, and refer used steering gear to higher authority.

e. Vehicle Pulls to Right or Left.
  (1) TIRES INFLATED UNEVENLY. Inflate tires properly (par. 108 a).

f. Vehicle Hard to Straighten Out After Turn to Right or Left.
  (1) IMPROPER TIRE INFLATION. Inflate tires to correct pressure (par. 108 a).

43. INSTRUMENTS.

a. Ammeter Inoperative.
  (1) WIRE DISCONNECTED OR BROKEN. Connect disconnected wire and splice or replace broken wire.
  (2) INTERNAL DEFECT. Replace ammeter (par. 115).

b. Speedometer Fluctuates and Jumps and/or is Noisy.
  (1) CABLE KINKED. Eliminate kinks, or replace cable, if permanently bent.
  (2) CABLE WORN AND BINDING. Replace cable.
  (3) SPEEDOMETER WORN. Replace speedometer.

c. Speedometer Inoperative.
  (1) CABLE DISCONNECTED. Connect cable (par. 100).
  (2) CABLE BROKEN. Replace cable.
  (3) DRIVE UNIT INOPERATIVE. Replace drive unit (par. 100).
  (4) INSTRUMENT INOPERATIVE. Replace speedometer (par. 115).

d. Oil Gage Does Not Register.
  (1) OIL PUMP INOPERATIVE OR ENGINE WITHOUT OIL PRESSURE FOR OTHER REASON. Stop engine and notify higher authority.

Bibliography

Books and reports

Blaine, Taylor, *Volkswagen Military Vehicles of the Third Reich: An Illustrated History* (Cambridge, MA, Da Capo Press, 2004)

British Intelligence Objectives Sub-committee, 'Part I: Report on Examination of German Light Aid Detachment Vehicle Type V.W. 82 "Volkswagen", the Rootes Group, Humber Ltd' (London, HM Stationery Office, 1946)

Busch, Reinhold, *Survivors of Stalingrad: Eyewitness Accounts from the Sixth Army, 1942–43* (Barnsley, Frontline, 2014)

Cooke, David, and Evans, Wayne, *Kampfgruppe Peiper: The Race for the Meuse* (London, Leo Cooper, 2005)

Director of Military Training, Army Service Forces, *The German Soldier* (US Army, 1944)

Guderian, Heinz (Foreword), *Blitzkrieg in their own Words: First-Hand Accounts from German Soldiers 1939–1940* (London, Amber Books, 2011)

Ludvigsen, Karl, *People's Car: An Investigation into the Design and Performance of Civilian and Military Volkswagens 1938–1946* (London, The Stationery Office, 1996.

Ludvigsen, Karl, *Professor Porsche's Wars: The Secret Life of Legendary Engineer Ferdinand Porsche Who Armed Two Belligerents Through Four Decades* (Barnsley, Pen & Sword, 2014)

Mayer-Stein, Hans-Georg, *Volkswagens of the Wehrmacht: German Vehicles in World War II* (Atglen, PA, Schiffer Military History, 1994)

Meyer, Hubert, *The 12th SS: The History of the Hitler Youth Panzer Division* (Mechanicsburg, PA, Stackpole, 2005)

Meyer, Kurt, *Grenadiers: The Story of Waffen SS General Kurt 'Panzer' Meyer* (Mechanicsburg, PA, Stackpole, 2005)

Oliver, Tony, *kfz.1 Kübelwagen Volkswagen Type 82* (London, Almark, 1978)

Piekalkiewicz, Janusz, *The Volkswagen Kübelwagen Type 82 in World War II* (Atglen, PA, Schiffer Military History, 2008)

SAE War Engineering Board, *German Amphibious Vehicle Supplement* (SAE War Engineering Board, August 1945)

Schreier, Konrad F. Jr (compiler), *VW Kübelwagen Military and Civilian 1940–90* (Cobham, Brooklands Books, 2008)

Seume, Keith, *The Beetle: A Comprehensive Illustrated History of the World's Most Popular Car* (Godalming, Colour Library Direct, 1997)

US Military Intelligence Service, 'Hints for Soldiers in Libya' in *Intelligence Bulletin* (December 1942)

US Military Intelligence Service, *German Winter Warfare* (Washington DC, War Department, 1943)

US Military Intelligence Service, 'German Light Amphibious Car', in *Intelligence Bulletin* (December 1944)

US War Department, TM E9-803, *German Volkswagen* (Washington DC, War Department, 6 June 1944)

Vollert, Jochen, *Kübelwagen on all Frontlines* (Erlangen, Tankograd Publishing, 2012)

Wehrmacht handbooks for the Le. Pkw K1 Typ 82 Kübelwagen
  D662/6 User Guide, 1941, reprint and translation by School of Tank Technology, Surrey, UK, 1942
  D662/7 Spare Parts List, OKH Berlin, May 1944
Wehrmacht handbooks for the Le. Pkw K2S Typ 166 Schwimmwagen
  D662/13 User Guide, Dec 1942
  D662/14 Spare Parts List, OKH Berlin, Mar 1943
  D699/41 Transparent Training Foils, Transart Berlin, Sep 1943

Magazines

Autocar
Custom Car

Index

Advertising and propaganda 12, 25, 82, 86-87
Afrika Korps (DAK) 17, 66, 68, 70, 73, 84
Ambi-Budd company 20, 22
Amphibious system 43-49, 110-114
    propulsion 46-49
    waterproofing 45-46
Audi 11
Austro-Daimler 12
Auto Union 11

Blaine, Taylor 21
Bodywork 12-14, 17, 21, 32, 37-41, 85, 91, 131
    canvas-top Beetle (Type 82/7) 17
    conversions 17
    grab handles 6, 70, 88, 107, 134
        document case 88
    intermediate-type 75
    open-top pick up (Type 82/5) 17
Brakes 35-37, 104, 114, 131, 151
    footbrake 35-37
    handbrake (parking) 35-38, 84, 105, 121, 152
British Intelligence Objectives Sub-Committee (BIOS) 6, 84
Bumper rod 38, 94
Bundeswehr 25
Busch, Reinhold 82-83

Camouflage 73, 75, 99, 117, 119, 122-123
Captured vehicles 23, 30, 82, 84-88, 91, 109, 116, 136
Center for Automotive Safety, Washington DC 92
    Malpractice Award 92-93
Chassis 12-14, 16, 20, 30, 37
Colour schemes 18, 106, 122
Combat crews 78-83, 98

Daimler 12
Daimler-Benz 11
    W3 12

D-Day invasion 74
DKW 11
Dodge, Lowell 92-93
Doors 40, 71, 92, 98
Drauz company 21
Drivers 98-101, 118, 120-121, 125
    licence 98-99
    proficiency badge 9
    training 99, 110
Driving area 30, 32, 90, 97, 101-103, 108, 117
    dashboard 32, 41, 91, 101-103, 106, 138
    heater (Type 181) 91
    instruments and controls 101-105, 107, 115, 152
    speedometer 102, 105
    steering wheel 97, 101
Driving characteristics and experience 107-110, 114-118
    amphibious 110-114
Dugdale, John 84, 115

Electrical systems and equipment 41-43, 104-105, 130, 138
    battery 41, 120-121, 123, 128-129, 133, 137, 149-150
    generator system 57-58
Ellis, H.E. 90-91
Engine compartment 33, 42, 80, 93, 129
    watertight 53
Engines 31-33, 51-59, 63, 92-93, 115, 127, 139, 142-144, 146
    access 31
    air-cooling and cleaning 12, 17, 25, 31-32, 51-52, 55-56, 58, 83, 131, 148
    air filter 51, 63
    crankcase and crankshaft 52-53
    flat-four 12
    installation 144
    location 32, 38
    pistons, camshaft and cylinders 53-54, 58, 146
    rear-mounted 25, 32, 83-84, 115

removal 143-144
    starting 52, 56-57, 59, 85, 103-104, 108, 123-124, 149
        cold-weather kit 56, 59, 123, 144
        by towing 133
    tune-up procedure 129
    ventilation 19
Enthusiasts 27
Europa Jeep 24
Exhaust system 22, 32, 112, 119, 124, 148

Feldgendarmerie 101
Fichtner, Ob. 13
First World War 10
Floor and frame 16, 30-31, 38, 40, 44, 85
Floorplans 11-12
Ford 11
Ford, Henry 13
Four-wheel drive 17, 21, 24-25, 62, 86, 92, 106, 109, 112-113
Front-wheel drive 31, 45
Fuel 56, 86, 120, 146
Fuel consumption 13, 17, 21, 101, 119-120, 123
    evaporation 136
Fuel system 131, 146-147
    carburettors 32, 52-53, 56, 124, 129, 138, 146
    filler caps 32, 38
    primer valve 52
    pump 57, 135
    stoppages 135
Fuel tanks and mounts 31-32, 43, 92, 101, 103, 138, 142, 146
    dipsticks 103
    spare cans 114

Gauglitz, Hauptmann 79
General Motors 11
German-Italian Panzer Armee 6
German Labour Front (DAF) 13
German light vehicles 114
Great Depression 10

Harcourt, Cyril 26
Heaters 133
Heer (German Army) 63, 67, 69, 114
Herzmer, Rudi 26
Himmler, Heinrich 19
Hitler, Adolf 10-12, 19, 21, 86
Hood (canvas) 19, 33, 41-42, 92, 131
Horch 11, 17
Horns 23, 41, 43, 48, 81, 104, 128
Hull 20, 31, 44-45, 109
HWA (Army Weapons Office) 13-14, 19, 21-22

Ignition system 41, 56-59, 102, 104, 123, 146, 148
   distributor 57, 128-129, 148
   spark plugs 58, 128-129, 148
Insignia and markings 9, 23, 68, 77, 83-84, 85-86, 125
Institute of Technology, Stuttgart 12
Instruction manuals (German) 37, 43-46, 48, 61, 107, 110, 120-124, 130, 136, 139-140
   Schwimmwagen 140

Jeeps (Wilys and Ford) 24, 31, 35, 41, 86-91, 93, 110, 117
   Amphibious (Sea) 88, 90-91

Komenda, Erwin 20
Kraft durch Freude (KdF) 13
Kübelwagen Type 82 6-7 et seq.
   Typ 82 aus Trop (tropical model) 18-19
   Type 82 rail conversion 139
   Type 157 rail-capable vehicle 18
   variants 17-18, 38
Kübelwagen name 14

Ledwinka, Hans 11-12
Liese, Albert 13
Liese, Kurt 13
Lighting 41-43, 104-105, 119, 149-150
   blackout lamps 41-42, 103
   direction indicators 41, 79, 102, 105, 119
   distance indicating lamp 41-43, 90
   headlights 29, 38, 41-42, 65-66, 132
   rear lamp 42, 80, 88, 90
Lubrication system 45-46, 54-55, 86, 114, 120, 123, 128, 131, 133, 136, 138, 146
   oil cooler system 57
   oiling points 55, 135

Luftwaffe 7, 69-70, 77, 81, 83, 87, 101, 125, 136

Maintenance and servicing 73, 86-87, 118, 123, 127-154
   At-halt service 130-132
   cold-climate 138-139
   environmental problems 132-133, 135-139
      condensation 136
      dust 118, 133, 135-137
      insects 121, 136
      rust 45, 136
   in-field servicing 129
   major components 139-140
   operational 128-132
   servicing schedule 128
   training 127
Materials used 30, 32, 38, 84
   rubber and fabric parts 119, 121
   shortage 22
Mercedes 12
Merscher, Helmut 78
Meyer, Kurt 79-81
Model, Gen. 73
Mudguards 38, 83, 86

Nader, Ralph 92
NATO 24, 26, 93
Noises 56, 90, 95, 130
NSDAP 10
NSKK 99
Number (registration) plates 7, 88, 90, 100

Opel 11
Operational conditions
   arctic (ice and snow) 108, 123-125, 138-139
   cross-country 63 , 69, 90, 118, 125
   desert 14, 37, 68, 72-73, 78, 98, 110, 118-121, 136
   in combat 71-75
   mountain terrain 74
   mud 109-110, 119, 122
   tropical 33, 120, 135-137
   winter 14, 80, 122-125, 128, 138
Operational theatres 17, 66, 74, 81, 118
   Ardennes 78, 82
   Balkans 67, 70, 74, 135
   Eastern Front (Soviet Russia and Ukraine) 14, 17, 23, 26-27, 66, 68-71, 73-74, 79-80, 82-84, 86, 107, 114, 121-123, 136, 138

France (Normandy) 22, 65, 68, 71, 75, 80-82, 84, 87, 91, 98-99, 103, 106-107, 111
Italy and Sicily 17, 67, 74-75, 114, 116-117, 128
North Africa 14, 17, 30, 66, 68, 70, 72, 74, 77-78, 83-85, 98, 110, 118-121, 135
Western Europe 17, 66, 68, 74
Yugoslavia 66-67, 72, 79, 81

Panzer divisions 23, 67-68, 70, 74, 78-80, 83, 115
Peiper, Ob. Joachim 74
Penhale, D. 94-95
Performance 30, 35, 51, 84, 91, 94-95, 110, 115, 119
   ground clearance 15, 17, 25, 93, 95, 108
   manoeuvrability 79, 82, 110
   off-road 13-14, 21, 24, 33, 87, 89, 93-95, 108, 112, 122
   on water 45
   road holding 108
   speed 18, 31, 79, 86-87, 108
   speed in water 21
   turning circle 109
Porsche Design Bureau 11-12, 19, 49
   Type 12 11-12
   Type 60 V3 12-13, 73
   Type 67 73
   Type 87 19, 133, 135
   Type 128 19, 21-22
Porsche, Dr. Ing. Ferdinand 10-12, 17, 19, 49
Porsche, Ferry 19, 21
Porsche, Stuttgart 22, 118
Prototype vehicles 14, 18-19
Production figures 7, 13, 17-18, 22-23, 27, 90
   post-war vehicles 90
Propeller unit and housing 20-23, 44-48, 69, 84, 90-91, 111-113, 127, 133, 139-140
   chain drive system 44
   removal 140

Railton, Arthur R. 92, 94
Rear-engine configuration 11, 115
Rear-wheel drive 31
Reflectors 94, 124
Reich Chancellory 13
Reichswehr 10
REME 116

Reports and allied analysis 83-90
 Autocar magazine 84, 90, 115, 116-117
 British Army Handbook 87 37-38, 84
 Custom Car Types 82 and 181 road test 91-92
 Humber/BIOS 6, 15, 31, 33-34, 36, 39-40, 55, 61, 84, 109, 118
 US Military Intelligence Service 120-122
  Schwimmwagen 21
 US Ordnance School 30
 US War Department TM E9-803 30-32, 34-35, 37, 56-57, 60-63, 84-85, 102, 108, 129-130, 138-139
 troubleshooting guide 146-154
 US SAE War Engineering Board 44, 87-88
 VW Safer Motoring 94-95
Restored vehicles 9, 18, 20, 23-24, 40, 55, 77, 83, 94-95, 106, 115
Ringhoffer-Tatra 12
Roles
 casualty evacuation 69-70, 73-74, 82
 command staff cars 17, 26, 68-70, 73, 99
 headquarters vehicles 67
 hunting car 23
 light ranging car 18
 medical vehicle 91
 mobile communications 74
 moving ammunition and supplies 74
 open-top pick-up (Type 82/5) 17
 post-war 23-24, 90-95
 radio car (Type 82/1) 17-18, 27, 30
 reconnaissance 67-69, 74, 78, 85
 repair cars 40
 signals car 18, 27
 siren car (Type 82/2) 17, 81
 troop transport 17
 utility cars 69
 workshop car 18
Rommel, Erwin 17, 70
Roos, Dr 70

Savings scheme 12-13
Schwimmwagen Type 166 6-7 *et seq.*
Seats 32, 38, 40-41, 90-91
Second World War 13, 23, 73, 77
Specifications 22
 capacities 35
 Kübelwagen 35
 Schwimmwagen 49

weight 14, 17, 21-22, 30, 37-38, 40-41, 44, 84, 88-90
Steering 30, 35, 43, 45, 48, 113, 131, 141, 152
 in water 44, 48, 90, 112-113
Steyr-Werke 12
Stowage 38, 40
 ammunition 76-77, 108
 rear cargo compartment 42-43, 76
Surviving vehicles 23, 95
Suspension 17, 26, 31, 33-34, 45-46, 84, 90, 93, 108, 115, 117, 131, 141
 front axle 34, 44, 131, 136, 150
 rear axle 36, 45, 60, 151
 shock absorbers 33-34, 45, 152
 torsion bar 12, 33-34

Targa Florio race 12
Tatra 12
Test driving and trials 13, 21-22, 94, 109, 112, 115, 117-118, 132-133
Todt, Fritz 10
Toolboxes and tools 33, 38, 40, 129
 blowtorch 132
 spade 41
Tow hook and towing 33, 132-133
Tracks vs. wheels 95, 122
Transmission and differential 31-32, 45, 47, 59-63, 108, 131, 150
 clutch 59-60, 62, 104, 147
 crawler gear 81, 83, 108
 driveshaft housing removal 36
 gearbox and gear lever 32, 45, 59-61, 90, 105, 115, 117, 139-142
 removal of gearbox and differential 140-142
 speed ratio 60
 Schwimmwagen 61
Trippel *Schwimkraftwagen* 20, 109
Trutz coachbuilders 14
Tyre pump 33, 130
Tyres 37, 48, 95, 114, 119, 131, 152
 balloon (sand/smooth) 14, 37, 110, 118-119
 cross-country 48
 in water 48
 low-profile 37, 48
 pressures 118, 121, 130, 152
 run-flat 21
 snow 92-93

Vehicle documents 100-101, 132
Vehicle Repair Stations 128

Versailles Treaty 10
Volkswagen (VW) 25
 Beach Buggies 27
 Beetle (Type 1) 9, 11-12, 25, 27, 91-92, 94
 Karmann Ghia (Type 1) 25
 KdF-Wagen 11, 13, 17, 21, 133, 135
 Microbus 25
 Transporter 25
 Type 181 (The Thing) 24-26, 91-94
 Type 183 Iltis 26
Volkswagen Australia 26-27
 Country Buggy (Type 197) 26-27, 91, 94-95
 Sakbayan 95
Volkswagen design bureau 13
Volkswagen Fallersleben/Wolfsburg factory 10, 13, 17, 22, 89
 forced labour 89
Volkswagen GmbH 12
Volkswagen of America 25
Vollert, Jochen 18
von Manstein, Gen. Erich 70

Waffen-SS 13, 22, 68-71, 74, 78-79, 85-86, 107, 133
Wanderer 11
Wartime production conditions 89
Weapons and fitments 75-78, 103, 113
 machine guns and mounts 22, 69, 75-79, 108, 134
  MG34 19, 69, 73, 75-77, 103, 116
  MG42 69, 75, 77, 116
  MP40 77
 rifles and mountings 40, 74, 76
  MP44 115
Wehrmacht 10, 13, 19, 67, 90, 101, 123-125
Wheels, hubs and bearings 33-34, 37, 128, 131, 150-152
 changing 36, 93, 116
 double rear 123
 rail 18, 139
 snow/skid chains 38, 69, 123
 spare 31, 42, 83, 87, 92
Windows (celluloid) 41, 49, 92, 107
Windscreen 37-38, 41, 112, 119, 125, 130, 132
Windscreen wipers 37, 43, 119, 125, 130

Zinßmeister, Ob. August 79
Zundapp 11